SpringerBriefs in Criminology

SpringerBriefs in Criminology present concise summaries of cutting edge research across the fields of Criminology and Criminal Justice. It publishes small but impactful volumes of between 50 and 125 pages, with a clearly defined focus. The series covers a broad range of Criminology research from experimental design and methods, to brief reports and regional studies, to policy-related applications.

The scope of the series spans the whole field of Criminology and Criminal Justice, with an aim to be on the leading edge and continue to advance research. The series will be international and cross-disciplinary, including a broad array of topics, including juvenile delinquency, policing, crime prevention, terrorism research, crime and place, quantitative methods, experimental research in criminology, research design and analysis, forensic science, crime prevention, victimology, criminal justice systems, psychology of law, and explanations for criminal behavior.

SpringerBriefs in Criminology will be of interest to a broad range of researchers and practitioners working in Criminology and Criminal Justice Research and in related academic fields such as Sociology, Psychology, Public Health, Economics and Political Science.

More information about this series at http://www.springer.com/series/10159

Georgios A. Antonopoulos ·
Andrea Di Nicola · Atanas Rusev ·
Fiamma Terenghi

Human Trafficking Finances

Evidence from Three European Countries

Springer

Georgios A. Antonopoulos
School of Social Sciences and Law
Teesside University
Middlesbrough, UK

Andrea Di Nicola
Faculty of Law
University of Trento
Trento, Italy

Atanas Rusev
Security Program
Centre for the Study of Democracy
Sofia, Bulgaria

Fiamma Terenghi
Faculty of Law
University of Trento
Trento, Italy

ISSN 2192-8533 ISSN 2192-8541 (electronic)
SpringerBriefs in Criminology
ISBN 978-3-030-17808-6 ISBN 978-3-030-17809-3 (eBook)
https://doi.org/10.1007/978-3-030-17809-3

This Springer imprint is published by the registered company Springer Nature Switzerland AG
The registered company address is: Gewerbestrasse 11, 6330 Cham, Switzerland

Acknowledgements

The study this *Springer Criminology Brief* is based upon was supported financially by the European Commission (Award reference: HOME/2015/ISFP/A0/4000008751). The authors would like to thank the participants of this study for their time and valuable insights, as well as Valentina Piol who, as an intern at eCrime (University of Trento), offered support during the study. The authors would also like to thank Georgios Papanicolaou and Parisa Diba for their comments on parts of the book.

Contents

About the Authors

Georgios A. Antonopoulos is Professor of criminology at Teesside University, UK.

Andrea Di Nicola is Associate Professor of criminology at the University of Trento, Italy.

Atanas Rusev is Senior Analyst (Security Programme) at the Centre for the Study of Democracy, Bulgaria.

Fiamma Terenghi is Research Fellow in criminology at the University of Trento, Italy.

Abbreviations

ACPO	Association of Chief Police Officers
CPS	Crown Prosecution Service
DDA	Direzione Distrettuale antimafia e antiterrorismo (National Antimafia and Antiterrorism Directorate)
EEA	European Economic Area
FATF	Financial Action Task Force
FISS	Financial Investigation Support System
FRONTEX	European Border and Coast Guard Agency
GAIN	Government Agency Intelligence Network
GDCOC	Directorate General Countering Organised Crime
GDP	Gross domestic product
GLAA	Gangmasters and Labour Abuse Authority
GRETA	Group of Experts on Action against Trafficking in Human Beings
HMRC	Her Majesty's Revenue and Customs
ICT	Information and communication technology
ILO	International Labour Organisation
JARD	Joint Asset Recovery Database
ML	Money laundering
MoI	Ministry of Interior
MPS	Metropolitan Police Service
MSHTU	Modern Slavery Human Trafficking Unit
NCA	National Crime Agency
NERSOU	North East Regional Special Operations Unit
NGO	Non-governmental organisation
NPIA	National Policing Improvement Agency
NRM	National Referral Mechanism
OCGs	Organised crime groups
OECD	Organisation for Economic Co-operation and Development
POCA	Proceeds of Crime Act
POCC	Proceeds of Crime Centre

RART	Regional Asset Recovery Team
ROCU	Regional Organised Crime Unit
SANS	State Agency National Security
SARs	Suspicious activity reports
SCDEA	Scottish Crime and Drug Enforcement Agency
SOCA	Serious and Organised Crime Agency
SPOC	Single point of contact
THB	Trafficking in human beings
UK	United Kingdom
UKBA	United Kingdom Border Agency
UKFIU	UK Financial Intelligence Unit
UKHTC	United Kingdom Human Trafficking Centre
UNTOC	United Nations Convention against Transnational Organised Crime

List of Figures

List of Tables

Introduction

Keywords Human trafficking · Sexual exploitation · Labour exploitation · Crime money · Information and communication technologies

Due to the nature and the increasing prevalence of trafficking in human beings, heavy emphasis has been paid to victims as they typically experience slavery-like conditions, serious abuse and even life-threatening situations. Victimisation has been a focal point of efforts by government agencies, NGOs and international organisations. As a result, two particular forms, sexual exploitation and labour exploitation, have become relatively more visible and thus detectable than other forms of human trafficking, such as organ removal (see, e.g., Andrees and Belser 2009; Antonopoulos and Papanicolaou 2018; UNODC 2018). Accounts on the trafficking of humans for sexual and labour exploitation have little to say about the proceeds generated from this criminal business. According to the Financial Action Task Force (FATF), in addition to its human costs, trafficking in human beings is considered as one of the most profitable criminal businesses with forced labour alone estimated to generate more than US$ 150 billion per year (FATF 2018). In addition, accounts on human trafficking are not typically concerned with the everyday nature and dynamics of criminal investment practices. In fact, although the literature on human trafficking and other illegal markets is booming, research on the financial management of these manifestations of 'organised crime' remains, with some notable exceptions, relatively limited (see, for instance, Reuter 1985; Moneyval 2005; Levi 2010; Petrunov 2011; Kruisbergen et al. 2012; Soudijn and Zhang 2013; Antonopoulos et al. 2018; Di Nicola and Terenghi 2016). One exception is the *Financing of Organised Crime* Projects (CSD 2015; 2018), which specifically focused on the processes and structures involved in financial management of the illegal tobacco trade, cocaine market and VAT fraud across European member states (see also Antonopoulos and Hall 2015), and human trafficking (CSD 2018). Another is the relatively sound understanding of finance-related issues in drug markets more generally (see Reuter et al. 1990; Naylor 2004; Brå 2007; Aziani 2018); existing work addresses prices, costs of doing business (Caulkins et al. 1999; Moeller 2012), investments and money laundering.

The gap in knowledge about financial management in the human trafficking business raises a series of key questions. What are the various forms and sources of financing in the human trafficking business? Which financial processes and practices are used by those involved in human trafficking? How do they settle payments? What (if any) interconnections exist between criminal structures involved in human trafficking and legitimate businesses or financial institutions? Do information and communication technologies (ICTs) offer enhanced financial opportunities for human traffickers, and, if so, in what way?

This book deals with these questions. The overall aim is to investigate the mechanisms of financial management in human trafficking in three selected European countries: Bulgaria, Italy and the UK. It addresses the ways in which capital is secured to allow human trafficking businesses to be initiated and sustained, how entrepreneurs and customers settle payments, the costs of conducting business in human trafficking, and how profits from the business are spent and invested. The chapter on Bulgaria focuses on sex trafficking, whereas the chapters on Italy and the UK provide accounts and data on both sex and labour trafficking.

"Trafficking" in this book follows the definition introduced by the Protocol to Prevent, Suppress and Punish Trafficking in Persons, especially Women and Children (Trafficking Protocol), supplementing the 2000 United Nations Convention against Transnational Organised Crime (UNTOC). According to article 3 of the Trafficking Protocol, trafficking in persons is *the recruitment, transportation, transfer, harbouring or receipt of persons, by means of the threat or use of force or other forms of coercion, of abduction, of fraud, of deception, of the abuse of power or of a position of vulnerability or of the giving or receiving of payments or benefits to achieve the consent of a person having control over another person, for the purpose of exploitation*. Exploitation includes, *at a minimum, the exploitation of the prostitution of others or other forms of sexual exploitation, forced labour or services, slavery or practices similar to slavery, servitude or the removal of organs* (United Nations 2000). The above definition of trafficking further involves two additional conditions: firstly, the consent of the exploited victim is irrelevant when the means specified in the definition have been used (art. 3(b)); secondly, the recruitment, transportation, transfer, harbouring or receipt of a person under the age of 18 (a child) constitute trafficking in persons, even if the particular means specified in the definition have not been used (art. 3(c)) (United Nations 2000).

While the UNTOC definition has served as the template for definitions of trafficking found in other pieces of national and international laws, such as the 2005 Council of Europe Convention on Action against Trafficking in Human Beings, or the UK Modern Slavery Act 2015 (which essentially aggregated "human trafficking" and "modern slavery"), it does not resolve with certainty key issues as they arise in the empirical manifestations of the phenomenon (see De Vries 2019). Firstly, the nature of the process leaves a considerable margin for uncertainty as to whether trafficking has *genuinely* taken place. From a victim-centred viewpoint, the process may result in a non-harmful outcome, even though an illegal situation exists (e.g. illegal prostitution or employment of adult migrants). According to the National Crime Agency (NCA), for example, 82% of potential victims exploited for labour in the UK in 2014 were European Economic Area (EEA) nationals *legally* entitled to live and work in the UK (NCA 2015). Secondly, from the viewpoint of the offending behaviour, the grey area concerns the element of organisation as defined in the main body of the UNTOC (i.e. art. 2(a): "structured group of three or more persons"). Engaging in the trafficking process does not require crossing such particular organisational threshold; in other words, trafficking may not always involve an "organised criminal group" (see Papanicolaou 2008; Oude Breuil et al. 2011; Siegel 2012; Weitzer 2012; Antonopoulos and Papanicolaou 2018). When trafficking is a "transnational" crime, it is best understood as a *process* embedded in contemporary migration flows facilitated by push, pull and facilitating factors and involving the availability of *at-risk population* in the countries of origin (see Van Liemt 2004; Europol 2011).

Each of the countries' case studies was based on the data gathered from a variety of sources. Firstly, open sources on the financing of organised crime in general and human trafficking in particular were reviewed. The review included academic articles and reports by research institutes, reports by governments, national and international law enforcement (Europol, national crime agencies, etc.) and international organisations (ILO, UNODC, FATF). Open sources included media sources and press releases from various law enforcement agencies. The available literature and open sources reviewed were in English, Bulgarian and Italian.

Secondly, statistical data on human trafficking were gathered from sources at the international and national levels. Where possible, data were collected from sources using a standardised methodology in order to ensure comparability. Thirdly, police files were utilised. This set of data included, among other, intelligence reports by the metropolitan police in the UK. These intelligence reports are essentially problem profiles on either human trafficking in particular or organised crime in general with the purpose to inform tactical tasking and coordinating groups within the police.

Finally, the most important source of data for the study included in-depth interviews with a variety of stakeholders related to human trafficking: experts (police officers, investigators, prosecutors, lawyers, criminologists/academic researchers working on the issue), victims of trafficking and (in the case of Bulgaria) criminal entrepreneurs. A total of 98 interviews were carried out in the three countries. In this book, the sources have been coded in order to preserve their anonymity. The first two letters of the code indicate the country ('BG' for Bulgaria; 'IT' for Italy; 'UK' for United Kingdom), 'E' indicates an expert, 'C' indicates a criminal entrepreneur/trafficker/exploiter, and "V" indicates a victim (Table 1).

The interviews were conducted implementing a common protocol (interview guide), which was designed to facilitate consistency of data collection and subsequent analysis of the different aspects of financial management of human trafficking. The interview protocol covered the same topics, including extent and nature of human trafficking, initial capital for financing of THB activities (market entry

Table 1 Number of interviewees, per type of interviewee

	Bulgaria	*Italy*	*UK*	**Total**
Experts (E)	29	24	20	73
Criminal entrepreneurs (C)	23	–	–	23
Victims (V)	–	1	1	2
				98

thresholds, sources of capital, access to external capital), criminal money management (type and structure of costs, forms and settlement of payments, handling of profits), role of the Internet and new ICT and their impact on financial management.

The respondents for the interviews were identified in three ways. Most of the interviewed experts were identified through official correspondence with government, judiciary and law enforcement bodies, as well as non-governmental organisations. Similarly, in order to conduct interviews with some criminal entrepreneurs in Bulgarian prisons, an official request to the prison administration was submitted and, subsequently, an informed consent from the inmates was obtained. Secondly, respondents were asked to recommend other relevant experts and, thus, through a snowball sampling additional interviewees were identified. The third method involved approaching participants from projects in the field of organised crime the authors had previously worked in. In many cases, the conducted interviews were supplemented and augmented through follow-up meetings and additional information acquired via phone or email correspondence.

The selected methods and data sources are not without limitations. Data retrieved through interviews with representatives of the authorities are often restricted by factors such as the level of competency and experience of the respondents, institutional priorities and broader political agendas. Another shortcoming of official accounts is a certain stereotyping of 'organised criminals', which eventually disregards the broader social and cultural context in which they operate (Hobbs & Antonopoulos, 2014). Similarly, interviews with criminal offenders are often burdened with issues such as accountability and validity of the information shared, as well as selection bias due to impossibility to assure representativeness of the interview sample, thus usually limiting the focus to criminal actors operating on small scale (e.g. Zhang & Chin, 2004). Media sources are also susceptible to various biases—they usually cover cases, which have been brought out to the public by the official authorities and, therefore, portray only 'success stories', not to mention the sensationalism and moralistic way of conveying the information. These characteristics substantially decrease the empirical value of media sources for analytical purposes (see Antonopoulos & Hall, 2015). The efforts to overcome the limitations of these data included triangulation of data through different sources. This allowed most dubious accounts to be eliminated and a certain level of data quality and robustness to be achieved.

Data collection in each country followed the common ethical standards for studies of a similar nature such as obtaining informed consent from each interviewee, ensuring confidentiality and protecting anonymity. Human rights, dignity and fundamental freedoms of all respondents were respected, and all personal data were handled according to national and EU data-protection legal frameworks.

Following this introduction, the book is based on three substantive chapters on human trafficking and its financial management in Bulgaria, Italy and the UK, respectively. Each of these chapters provides: firstly, a general overview of the human trafficking business; secondly, an account of the social organisation of human trafficking and the key actors involved; and, thirdly, the financial aspects of human trafficking in terms of sources of financing, settlement of payments, costs of business, profits made and how the profits are spent and further invested, as well as an account of the role the Internet plays in the human trafficking business and its finances. Slight differences in the format in which the material is presented in this book are due to the differential approach taken by researchers in Bulgaria, Italy and the UK, access to relevant actors, as well as differences in the amount of relevant literature per country. The book ends with a concluding chapter, which synthesises the accounts offered in chapters one, two and three.

References

Andrees, B. & Belser, P. (Eds.). (2009). *Forced labour: Coercion and exploitation in the private economy*. Boulder, Co.: Lynne Rienner Publishers.

Antonopoulos, G. A. & Hall, A. (2015). The financial management of the illicit tobacco trade in the United Kingdom. *British Journal of Criminology*. https://doi.org/10.1093/bjc/azv062

Antonopoulos, G. A. & Papanicolaou, G. (2018). *Organised crime: A very short introduction*. Oxford: Oxford University Press.

Antonopoulos, G. A., Hall, A., Large, J., Shen, A., Crang, M., & Andrews, M. (2018). *Fake goods, real money*. Bristol: Policy Press.

Aziani, A. (2018). *Illicit financial flows: An innovative approach to estimation*. New York: Springer.

Brå. (2007). *Where did all the Money go?* Report 2007:4. Stockholm: Brå.

Caulkins, J. P., Johnson, B., Taylor, A., & Taylor, L. (1999). What drug dealers tell us about their costs of doing business. *Journal of Drug Issues*, *29*(2), 323–340.

CSD. (2015). *Financing of organised crime*. Sofia: Centre for the Study of Democracy.

CSD. (2018). *Financing of organised crime—Human trafficking in focus*. Sofia: Centre for the Study of Democracy.

De Vries, I. (2019). Connected to crime: An exploration of the nesting of labour trafficking and exploitation in legitimate markets. *British Journal of Criminology*, *59*, 209–230.

Di Nicola, A. & Terenghi, F. (2016). Managing finances in the illicit tobacco trade in Italy. *Trends in Organized Crime*, *19*(3–4), 254–272.

Europol. (2011). *Trafficking in human beings in the European Union*. The Hague: Europol.

FATF (Financial Action Task Force). (2018). *Financial flows from human trafficking*. Paris: FATF-APG.

Hobbs, D. & Antonopoulos, G. A. (2014). How to research organised crime. In L. Paoli (Ed.), *The Oxford handbook of organised crime* (pp. 96–117). New York: Oxford University Press.

Kruisbergen, E. W., Van de Bunt, H. G., & Kleemans, E. R. (2012). *Georganiseerde criminaliteit in Nederland. Vierde rapportage op basis van de Monitor Georganiseerde Criminaliteit*. Den Haag: Boom Juridische Uitgevers.

Levi, M. (2010). Preceeds of crime: Fighting the financing of terrorism. *Criminal Justice Matters, 81*(1), 38–39.

Moeller, K. (2012). Costs and revenues in street level cannabis dealing. *Trends in Organised Crime, 15*(1), 31–46.

Moneyval. (2005). *Proceeds from trafficking in human beings and illegal migration*. Strasbourg: Council of Europe.

Naylor, R. T. (2004). *Wages of crime*. Ithaca, NY: Cornell University Press.

NCA. (2015). *NCA strategic assessment: The nature and scale of human trafficking in 2014*. London: NCA.

Oude Breuil, B., Siegel, D., van Reenen, P. Roos, L., & Beijer, A. (2011). Human trafficking revisited: The legal, law enforcement and ethnographic narrative on sex trafficking to Western Europe. *Trends in Organised Crime, 14*(1), 30–46.

Papanicolaou, G. (2008). The sex industry, human trafficking and the global prohibition regime: A cautionary tale from Greece. *Trends in Organised Crime, 11*(4), 379–409.

Petrunov, G. (2011). Managing money acquired from human trafficking. *Trends in Organised Crime, 14*, 165–183.

Reuter, P. (1985). *The organisation of illegal markets*. Washington, D.C.: National Institute of Justice.

Reuter, P., MacCoun, R., & Murphy, P. (1990). *Money from crime*. Washington, DC: RAND.

Siegel, D. (2012). Mobility of sex workers in European cities. *European Journal on Criminal Policy and Research, 18*, 255–268.

Soudijn, M. R. J. & Zhang, S. X. (2013). Taking loansharking into account: A case study of Chinese vest-pocket lenders in Holland. *Trends in Organised Crime, 16*, 13–30.

United Nations. (2000). *Protocol to prevent, suppress and punish trafficking in persons, especially women and children, supplementing the United Nations convention against transnational organized crime*. Adopted by UN General Assembly resolution A/RES/55/67 of 15 November 2000).

UNODC. (2018). *Global report on trafficking in persons, 2018*. New York: UNODC.

Van Liemt, G. (2004). *Human trafficking in Europe: An economic perspective*. Geneva: ILO.

Weitzer, R. (2012). Sex trafficking and the sex industry: The needs for evidence-based theory and legislation. *Journal of Criminal Law and Criminology, 101*(4), 1337–1370.

Zhang, S. & Chin, K.-L. (2004). *Characteristics of Chinese human smugglers*. Washington, D.C.: U.S. Department of Justice.

Chapter 1
Human Trafficking and Its Financial Management in Bulgaria

1.1 Introduction

Trafficking in human beings (THB) for the purpose of sexual exploitation is considered one of the largest Bulgarian criminal markets since the beginning of the new millennium (CSD 2012). After the lifting of Schengen visas for Bulgarian nationals in 2001, Bulgaria became a major country of origin for the trafficking in human beings exploited in the EU. The existing research on THB and prostitution in Bulgaria indicates that these criminal activities not only generate huge incomes for Bulgarian organised crime but also has detrimental social and economic impact on local communities (Bezlov et al. 2016; CSD 2007, 2012). The victims of THB in Bulgaria are mainly women trafficked for sexual exploitation, but other enduring criminal networks involved in trafficking for forced labour, sham marriages, forced begging and pickpocketing have also been detected, as well as criminal networks involved in trafficking of pregnant women for the purpose of selling their new-born babies (GRETA 2016).

Recognising the extent of the problem of trafficking, Bulgaria has expanded and sharpened its legislation during the last 15 years. Human trafficking was first introduced as a separate offence in the Criminal Code for the first time in 2002, following the ratification of the Palermo Protocol. The new articles generally adhered to the definition laid down in the protocol and addressed both national and trans-border trafficking in human beings. However, in contrast to many European countries, Bulgaria criminalises trafficking irrespective of the consent of the victim, viewing the use of any special means such as coercion or the giving of benefits as aggravating circumstances (ПРБ 2010). Since their adoption, the Criminal Code articles have been amended and complemented in 2009 and 2013 to incorporate additional types of trafficking such as trafficking of pregnant women with the purpose of selling their new-born babies and trafficking for forced begging. The latest amendments were

G. A. Antonopoulos et al., *Human Trafficking Finances*, SpringerBriefs
in Criminology, https://doi.org/10.1007/978-3-030-17809-3_1

introduced as a result of the harmonisation of the Bulgarian legislation with the 2011 EU Directive on Human Trafficking.[1]

Since 2007, when Bulgaria and Romania joined the European Union, and especially since 2013, when the restrictions on the access of the two countries to the common EU labour market were removed, THB related processes have undergone a significant transformation. The freedom to travel to and legally work in EU member states has barred criminal networks from controlling victims' access to the common European labour market, including that of sexual services. In addition, as European and Bulgarian law enforcement and judiciary bodies have stepped up cooperation with their counterparts on an international scale, criminal networks have become less likely to use violence against THB victims and, therefore, less efficient in recruiting new victims or exploiting already recruited victims. The socio-demographic changes such as the smaller number of children born after 1990 and migration towards big cities have also contributed to shrinking the pool of persons vulnerable to THB (Bezlov et al. 2016).

The criminal networks evolved also in their attempt to adapt to the changing environment, going through several stages shaping their characteristics. The first period of criminal networks' development began in the mid-1990s when the trafficking of women for sexual exploitation was strongly linked to the domestic prostitution market. During this period, the large criminal syndicates of the so called "violent insurers"[2] turned the sex market into an important source of revenue, establishing control over supply through ownership of hotels, nightclubs and bars in major cities and resorts. Use of violence, often in extreme forms, was widespread (CSD 2007).

With the lifting of Schengen visas, which marks the start of the second period, Bulgarian criminal organisations already established in some of the member states could dramatically expand their prostitution business. Initially, it was the big criminal players—local units of the so called "violent insurers" in Bulgarian cities—that made use of this opportunity. Later, some independent procurers and networks stepped in the cross-border trafficking as well. In this period, THB for sexual exploitation became the largest source of revenue for organised crime and Bulgaria, albeit a small country, became the second or third biggest country of origin for THB victims in a number of EU states (Bezlov et al. 2016; CSD 2012).

The third period started after the initial post-accession period (2007–2009). Bulgarian criminal networks rapidly adapted to changing conditions. Patterns for controlling THB victims started to rely primarily on non-violent methods and economic inducement. The big criminal syndicates were largely replaced by loose networks with flexible arrangements and frequently changing composition of actors, although

[1]Directive 2011/36/EU of the European Parliament and of the Council of 5 April 2011 on preventing and combating trafficking in human beings and protecting its victims, and replacing Council Framework Decision 2002/629/JHA, OJ L 101, 15.4.2011.

[2]The so called "violent insurers" or *grupirovki* were the first powerful organised crime groups in Bulgaria, which emerged in the early 1990s and started their criminal activities with a wide use of violence and extortion. Most of them established private security and insurance companies as fronts for their extortion. Subsequently, most of them developed extensive crime portfolios including drug distribution, prostitution, contraband, etc.

hierarchically structured organisations did not disappear. On the other hand, sex workers in the different EU member states became less and less dependent on organised crime infrastructure and logistics (Bezlov et al. 2016).

Given the overwhelming prevalence of the trafficking for sexual exploitation in Bulgaria, the analysis below focuses exclusively on this type of trafficking and its financial management inside and outside the country. The THB for sexual exploitation is deeply interwoven with the domestic and foreign prostitution markets and during the collection of data and its analysis it became apparent that it is almost impossible to distinguish between these two phenomena. Much has been written on the problem of trafficking in human beings in Bulgaria. However, one of the least explored aspects of this nefarious phenomenon remains its financial aspects, as well as the business models of the criminal groups behind it.

1.2 Market Overview

According to the Prosecutor's Office of Bulgaria, 90% of the victims of trafficking for the period 2005–2016 have been female (ПРБ 2017). Trafficking for labour exploitation is the second most common type of THB, but it is significantly less common, with only 12% of pre-trial proceedings in the period 2011–2015 dealing with this type of trafficking (GRETA 2016). The data from Bulgaria corresponds to the Europol assessment for EU countries whereby organised crime groups (OCGs) involved in THB for purposes other than sexual exploitation is about 10% (Europol 2016).

During the last 10 years, there were several attempts to estimate the number of sex workers and respectively the scale of both cross-border and domestic trafficking in human beings. The first assessment of cross-border THB estimated that the number of Bulgarian sex workers abroad was between 8000 and 18,000 in the period 2003–2007 (CSD 2007). The second estimate on the scale of cross-border trafficking referred to the period 2005–2009 and indicated that between 11,000 and 21,000 sex workers from Bulgaria worked in other EU countries and generated about €1.5 billion, which is roughly equal to 2.6–2.7% of the national GDP for the same period. Roughly, half of these proceeds are controlled by the Bulgarian organised crime (CSD 2012). The most recent threat assessment on serious and organised crime in Bulgaria for the period 2012–2017 arrived at similar estimates (CSD 2018). Estimates on the revenues of the domestic sex market also vary—according to the estimations in 2007, the number of sex workers in Bulgaria was 5000–6000 and the generated revenues amounted at €115–120 million (CSD 2007). The second assessment estimated the internal market at €123–€205 million generated by 6000–10,000 sex workers (CSD 2012). The most recent assessment indicated €115–€135 million revenues generated by the domestic market (CSD 2018).

The public data from several EU member states reveal a dwindling number of victims from Bulgaria since 2012. The Dutch and German data on recorded THB victims indicate that the number of victims from Bulgaria in 2016 was 50% lower

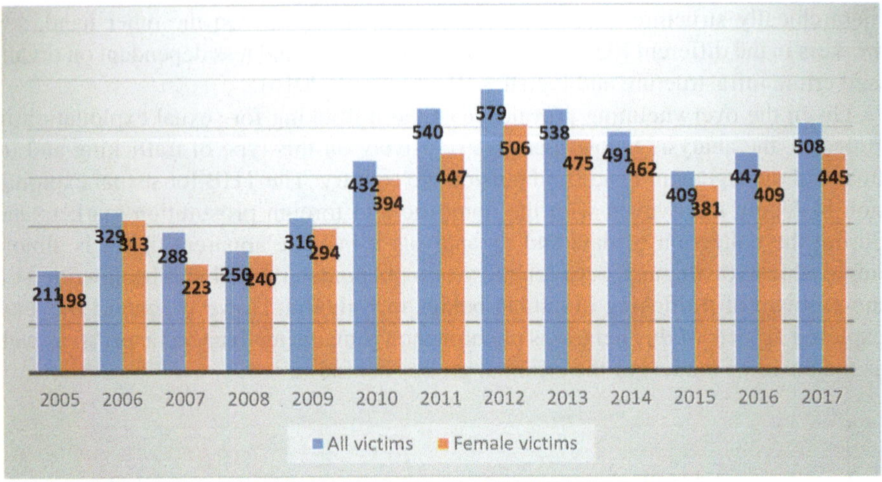

Fig. 1.1 Victims of trafficking involved in pre-trial proceedings, 2005–2017. *Source* Prosecutor's Office data

than in 2012 (Nationaal Rapporteur 2017). Similarly, the German data shows that the number of Bulgarian victims of THB for sexual exploitation have decreased by 49% in 2015 compared to 2012 (BKA 2016). At the same time, the number of victims identified by the Bulgarian authorities remains stable (see Fig. 1.1). According to the latest GRETA report, for the period 2011–2015 the number of victims of domestic trafficking in Bulgaria is roughly equal to the number of victims of cross-border trafficking (GRETA 2016).

However it should be noted that domestic trafficking and cross-border trafficking are interlinked and in many cases appear to be simply stages of one and the same criminal activity (CSD 2007, 2012; Риск Монитор 2010). Often, following the recruitment, the victims are initially exploited within the country. Common destinations for newly recruited victims are Sofia, Varna and Bourgas or some of the summer or winter resorts depending on the season. At a later stage they are trafficked and exploited abroad, but their traffickers periodically return and exploit them at home as well. Nevertheless, due to the increasingly easier access to the sex market in the EU, a growing number of victims start working abroad, without prior exploitation at the domestic prostitution market (see next section for further details).

At the time the interviews for this report were conducted, the number of THB victims was deemed to be on the decline judging from the observed significant decrease in the new investigations initiated by the Prosecutor's Office. The number of the new proceedings plummeted from 141 in 2012 to 86 in 2017 (ПРБ 2013, 2018). However, closer examination of the factors behind this suggested a somewhat different dynamic. Apparently, several factors related to law enforcement institutions have contributed to this significant drop in the investigations in the last 5 years. The most significant impact had the restructuring of the Directorate General Countering Organ-

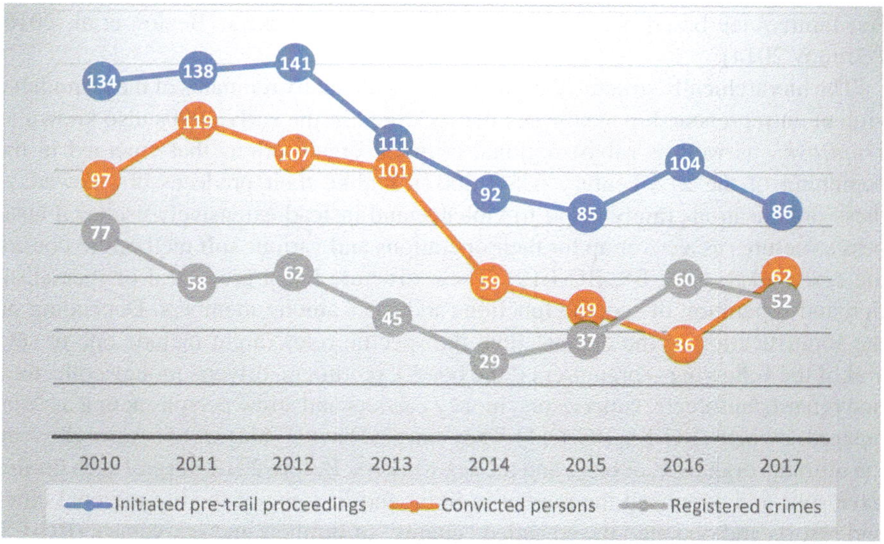

Fig. 1.2 Registered crimes, pre-trial proceedings and convicted offenders for THB, 2010–2017. *Source* Prosecutor's Office annual reports, MoI annual statistics (2010–2017)

ised Crime (GDCOC), the agency most actively involved in THB investigations. The agency went through two major reorganisations during the period 2012–2015, which led to an abrupt suspension of numerous ongoing investigations and loss of momentum (BG-E12, BG-E14, BG-E20, BG-E23, BG-E24). These institutional reforms coincided with the restructuring of the Public Prosecutor's Office and the establishment of new Specialised Prosecution Service in 2012, which additionally contributed to the decrease in the number of the initiated pre-trial proceedings (see Fig. 1.2).

1.3 Market Structure and Social Organisation of Trafficking Networks

Once extensively controlled by organised crime and practically cartelised in all big cities and resorts, the prostitution market in Bulgaria is now rather fragmented and decentralised. Similar tendencies have been reported for cross-border trafficking (Bezlov et al. 2016; CSD 2012; Стойчев 2016). Despite the fragmentation of the prostitution market and the increased share of independent actors, the human trafficking business in the country and abroad still remains largely controlled by Bulgarian organised crime. Since the 1990s, no criminals from other nationalities have ever had noticeable presence in the country or played any role in cross-border trafficking. Generally, the following profiles of sets of actors can be distinguished: hierarchically structured organisations; loose networks of collaborating independent traffickers; family/clan-based organisations; independent traffickers (Bezlov et al. 2016; Petrunov 2014).

The hierarchically structured organisations are usually remnants of the formidable violent entrepreneurship syndicates that emerged in the early 1990s also known as *grupirovki*, as well as robust regional criminal organisations that emerged in the beginning of the 21st century (CSD 2007). Unlike their predecessors, nowadays these organisations rarely resort to violence and instead extensively use legal business structures as a cover up for their operations and various soft methods to control the sex workers (BG-E5, BG-E19). Their structure has a great deal of specialisation and separation of specific functions and roles among members. Depending on the sophistication of the organisation, the specific roles might include one or several of the following—organisers ("the boss"), recruiters, drivers, money collectors, bodyguards/enforcers, supervisors, money carriers and straw persons acting as legal business owners (BG-E5, BG-E11). They can also have 3–4 layers of control between the ultimate organiser, or boss, and the sex workers. Before 2012, several such groups have split and cartelised the market in Sofia and in some of the big regional cities and resorts and operated the so called "chains" of brothels and sex venues (BG-E5, BG-E6).

The accession of Bulgaria to the EU in 2007, the targeted law enforcement pressure on the market in the period 2010–2012, and the increasing use of information and communication technologies (ICT) in the prostitution markets have to a large extend reduced the opportunities for cartelisation and control over the prostitution markets. Whereas in the past these organisations were exerting control on the access to the market by coercion and enforcing protection fees to all independent actors, nowadays they would rather contract the sex workers as employees and exert control through the use of market mechanisms, such as providing access to profitable locations or venues, and securing protection against rival competition and police authorities (BG-E17, BG-E25). Other similar arrangements include striking deals with independent traffickers for granting access to their locations or venues for a fee. The fee may include advanced payment and a commission based on the earnings of the sex workers, who are allowed to work in their venues. Depending on the size and sophistication of the organisation, its leaders might have invested in venues both in Bulgaria and abroad, while other have opted only for a single venue either in Bulgaria or abroad (BG-E11, BG-E21).

The loose networks usually comprise of several independent traffickers, wherein each of them independently recruits women from Bulgaria or elsewhere, as a rule with their consent, and secure a location for them. Each procurer would also provide his sex workers with protection from violent clients, secure lodging and clients, arrange residence permits, licenses and resolve other administrative issues. Lately, traffickers have even been communicating with clients online, mostly via social networks. To ward off competition, the procurer resorts to his network of friends and compatriots. Under this modus operandi, each trafficker takes care of all aspects related to the business and this allows him to recruit two or three girls at a time. There are also some examples of procurers managing 3–4 girls in different EU countries who are not aware of each other. When looking for new girls, he entrusts guardianship over the prostitute to friends from his network and returns the favour when asked by another network member (BG-E20, BG-E27, and BG-E29). Procurers often marry the prostitute to avoid getting involved with the police (BG-E5). However, this type of arrangement works out rarely as conflicts often arise among traffickers, since competition for better venues and high-earning sex workers is fierce (BG-E19, BG-E20).

Family/clan based organisations are typical for traffickers from the Roma community, where usually members of the organised crime group are part of the extended family. The structure usually follows the familial links with an elder authority at the top of the organisation and specific tasks divided between the members of the family. These organisations usually traffic women from the same ethnic group and even other family members. In some cases, they also resort to buying women from other groups or networks (BG-E5, BG-E11, BG-E13, BG-E14).

The independent traffickers are usually a couple (married or not) or a trafficker with 2–3 sex workers, who operate as a family/small business. The women solicit customers and provide sexual services, while the men provide protection and facilitation. Independent traffickers do not share their earnings with some criminal organisation but may pay a fixed fee to them in order to obtain the right to work at a particular location. Thus they keep all the revenues for themselves, but risk extortion demands and violent assaults from other competitors or being reported to local authorities as there is no group or network to protect them (BG-E17, BG-E26).

All types of trafficking organisations use the same strategy to reduce risk of detection and apprehension by the police, which involves acquiring consent of the exploited women and pre-negotiating the division of their earnings, using violence in exceptional cases, and often posing as their friends or spouses. On the other hand, the collected data indicates that criminal networks involved in trafficking offer sex workers both economic and safety advantages. Women who try to work on their own appear to be more likely to become victims of violent incidents or to earn less because of their limited access to profitable locations in central and western Europe where demand for sex services is high (BG-E19, BG-E22).

1.3.1 Structure of the Domestic Sex Market

The extent of involvement and modus operandi of these sets of trafficking actors both at the domestic prostitution market and the prostitution markets abroad varies among the different market segments. The domestic prostitution market in Bulgaria can generally be divided among three main segments—outdoor, indoor and high-end prostitution (Bezlov et al. 2016; CSD 2012). The market segments can be distinguished based on the place where the sex services are provided, the price range, and the clientele. Similar division can also be applied to the prostitution markets abroad, although the price brackets differ from country to country.

The lowest market segment in Bulgaria is outdoor prostitution, which comprises of sex workers who offer sex services mostly in public, open spaces. One group focuses on frequented places in big cities such as railway and bus stations, bridges, shoddy hotels, byways and side alleys parallel to main streets. Some of them migrate to the outskirts of resorts during the tourist seasons. The second group works along highways, main roads and the roads close to border crossings, mostly at parking lots, motels, crossroads and the like. Their main clients are truck drivers. The prices of both groups are rather low, ranging from €5 to €15 per client. Depending on the locations, prostitutes can service from 3–5 to 10–20 clients daily. The sex workers in this segment are recruited from various socially disadvantaged groups, mostly from Roma neighbourhoods (CSD 2007; Стойчев 2016). Each neighbourhood serves as a supply source for a particular region in Bulgaria. Other such pools are heroin addicts, young women raised at institutions or extremely poor families.

This segment is mostly occupied by the family-based organisations from the Roma ethnicity, as well as some independent traffickers. In the past, some hierarchically structured organisations that strived to monopolise or at least cartelise the prostitution market in their cities were imposing protection fees on the procurers operating in this segment for the right to operate at a given location. Currently the practice for levying protection fees continues, although monopolies and oligopolies at prostitution markets in the capital and in the regional cities seized to exist. This niche is taken over in some regions by poly-criminal organisations that are involved in a variety of other criminal activities such as drug dealing, extortion, human smuggling, etc. Procurers and the sex workers are usually charged a set fee, which has ranged from €10–€15 per day to €50–€100 per week at different times (BG-E19, BG-E22).

The largest number of sex workers operates in the indoor prostitution segment, which can be provisionally divided in several substrata. The bottom one is occupied by the so called "apartment prostitution" named after the habitual locations where sex services are preformed—rented flats on the first floors of residential buildings. Prices vary depending on the town from €30 to €50[3] per hour of standard sex. VIP or escort clubs occupy the next substratum at which prices are higher and control over prostitutes is more lenient. The segment also includes the escort services. The average prices range from €50 to €75 per hour of standard sex. The most luxurious substratum comprises erotic bars and adult clubs. Sex workers at such erotic bars take in additional revenue in the form of soliciting drinks from customers and dancing. The owners of such venues as a rule pre-select the sex workers before contracting them and tend to regularly replace them with new ones. Standard sex average prices range between €150 and €250 per hour.

Brothels and other sex venues are usually located in big cities, although other popular locations are resorts and border towns. Part of the sex workers who work in the biggest cities migrate to coastal resorts from June to September and to mountain ones from December to March. Usually owners of sex venues in some of the big cities also keep such venues at the resorts, so the sex workers are moved from the big cities to the resorts and back. Border prostitution in towns such as Svilengrad

[3]These prices are given as an example however, in the last few years prices have consistently increased countrywide.

at the Turkish border and Sandanski and Petrich near the Greek border also takes place predominantly in various bars and hotels and the clients are predominantly foreigners.

The sex venues have their own internal rules and the workers that breach them bear financial penalties. The number of sites belonging to the indoor prostitution segment in Sofia, for example, has varied throughout the years depending on the demand for sex services and the extent of law enforcement pressure over criminal groups. The number of flats and clubs in Sofia, for instance, has ranged between 100 and 300, of VIP clubs from 20 to 30, and of erotic bars from 10 to 20 (BG-E19, BG-E22).

This market segment is dominated by hierarchical groups, who usually invest in sex venues at lucrative locations—in the city centre of Sofia or some of the big cities, as well as in the coastal and mountain resorts. However, in the period 2010–2012 the controlled chains of apartment brothels in big cities disappeared giving way to independently working (mostly in pairs) prostitutes renting their own living space, increasingly offering their services online, and occasionally paying criminal networks security fees to guard them against possible threats from clients. Many independent procurers have also started to operate in this market segment running apartments with their own sex workers or providing call girl services with extensive use of online advertising. Hierarchical groups used to levy protection fees on such actors in the past but after 2012 a significant number of independent procurers ceased paying for protection. The attempts to re-establish monopoly over certain markets, e.g. Varna, have not succeeded due to law enforcement pressure and resistance from the other local groups (BG-E12, BG-E18).

The high-end prostitution market segment accommodates various legal business structures that are used as cover for offering exclusive sex services. Typical businesses used in this market segment include fashion, model and advertising agencies, as well as talent managing companies working with dance troupes and pop folk performers. These bogus fashion agencies hire young women as models under a permanent or temporary contract to participate in fashion shows, advertising campaigns, TV shows, product promotions, movies, magazine photo sessions, etc., for a particular fee. However, many of the women are enticed to perform sex services and thus the line between their duties as fashion models and escorts becomes blurred. The price of sex is €500 and over, but as collected data indicates, the financial side is often less important for the criminal organisations compared to the opportunity to influence the political and business elites in Bulgaria. This segment is also dominated by hierarchical organisations, which in many cases also have presence in the indoor segment (BG-E6, BG-E12, BG-E18).

1.3.2 The Organisation of the Cross-Border Trafficking

The structure and functioning of the cross-border trafficking closely resembles the domestic prostitution market. Street sex workers would be commissioned to work on selected streets, parking lots and open spaces in large European cities. Sex workers in the indoor segment are exploited in a variety of sex venues such as brothels, hotels, sex clubs, bars and windows, and the like after traffickers negotiate access with the respective owners or criminal organisations that controls them. Criminal organisations operating at the high-end prostitution level solicit foreign clients during the modelling agencies' tours abroad, usually in neighbouring countries such as Greece and Turkey, more exclusive destinations such as Dubai, and less often in Italy and France. Subsequently the sex workers are secured engagements in thematic or weekend parties, and business conferences (BG-E19, BG-E22).

Some of the big hierarchical organisations operate both at the domestic and foreign prostitution markets. However, the regional trafficking networks in most cases do not have presence at the domestic market, but prefer to organise only cross-border trafficking to EU countries, Switzerland or Norway. They recruit sex workers from the towns they are based or the nearby smaller towns and commission them to particular European cities. Criminal organisations and networks from Bulgarian cities such as Sliven, Pazardzhik, Stara Zagora, Haskovo, Pleven, Ruse, Dobrich, Vidin, etc., have established trafficking channels to Brussels, Strasbourg, Rotterdam, Oslo, Cologne, Vienna, Valencia, Rome, Koblenz, etc. To escape dependence and payment of protection fees, the regional procurement networks operate independently from the big hierarchical organisations, when supplying sex workers to the EU (BG-E20, BG-E29).

The big hierarchical organisations with established presence on the domestic market, on the other hand, have a different business model that guarantees better control over the sex workers. The newly recruited women first work in some of the bigger Bulgarian cities or resorts and after proving their loyalty and accountability are commissioned to more profitable locations abroad (BG-E19, BG-E27, BG-E29). The sex workers periodically return to work back in Bulgaria upon completion of a certain period or whenever some problem arises (e.g. extortion demands from other criminal groups, conflicts with competitors, police operations, etc.). In contrast, the sex workers trafficked by the regional networks would usually have between-jobs spells at home or sometimes work at a brothel owned by the group with domestic presence.

As the interviews suggest, the opportunities of the Bulgarian traffickers to participate in the EU sex market and specifically in the outdoor and the indoor segment have widened with time. At the start of the century the newly formed regional hierarchical groups and loose networks would stick to a certain European city or region, which they get to know well and subsequently they started to expand to new cities, thus doubling the number of trafficking destinations in recent years (BG-E19, BG-E21). Whereas in the past, a few big organisations and networks controlled the trafficking channels, currently various trafficking organisations started to invest abroad in order to exert direct control of the victim's workplace by purchasing/renting sites such as bars, restaurants, hotels, night clubs, windows, escort websites, escort companies, etc. This strategy involves establishing of legal business structures as a front of their operations and along with the advantages of enhanced form of control over the victims, it also offers them the opportunity to better shield their activities from police scrutiny (BG-E19, BG-E22).

1.4 Financing and Financial Management

1.4.1 Source of Capital for Initiating/Sustaining Criminal Operations. Access to Capital in Critical Moments

Many of the interviewed traffickers in the present study claim that no initial investment is needed to enter the market of THB for sexual purposes (BG-C13, BG-C14, BG-C17, BG-C20, BG-C3, BG-E9). However, entering the prostitution market can have different forms—from simple procuring of a victim to a close circle of acquaintances to securing a profitable location in some brothel abroad. While the former may not bear any financial costs, the latter appears to require initial investments. For example, some of the interviewed offenders mention that in the indoor segment securing access to a profitable location for a sex worker in Bulgaria can cost from €1000–€3700 (BG-C3, BG-C7) and abroad from €2000–€4000 (BG-C4, BG-C7).[4] In addition to that they also disclose costs for recruitment, transportation and lodging. Certainly larger investments are needed if a trafficker aims at becoming an owner or manager of a brothel or other sex venue. For example, one of the interviewees indicated that the rent of an adult club at the Bulgarian coast for the summer season amounts at €60,000, due in advance (BG-E3). More profitable establishments in Western Europe certainly cost a lot more; for example, one of the interviewed police officer reported that a trafficker invested one million euros to purchase an adult club in Spain (BG-E21).

Collected data indicates that in many cases social ties and networks are being converted into quantifiable value, whereby initial capital for a market entry, or a market expansion is loaned to the newcomer from actors who are already established in the trafficking for sexual exploitation, be it friends or extended family members (BG-C10 and BG-C7 for expansion; BG-C2 for entry). Accounts of social ties, connections, friends and extended family that factor in the genesis of human trafficking endeavours abound in the data collected from the respondents. At least three instances reveal that being part of the wider network of traffickers for sexual purposes exposes the members to opportunities for lines of quick credit with preferential interest rates when borrowing from "colleagues" (BG-C8, BG-C6, BG-C5). Being connected to people in the business, which entails trust and mutual assistance for starting up appears to be a crucial element in facilitating initial expenditures and diminishing or removing altogether barriers to market entry. The prevailing model for starting up is epitomised by a statement from one of the respondents that highlights the importance of social networks and social capital: "if you have a girl ready to go right from the start, every trusted person will help you out" (BG-C10).

In this regard collected data is in line of the existing literature on the importance of social capital for a market entry. Whereas opportunities for most conventional crimes are countless, the sophistication of its activities makes organised crime opportunities

---

[4]The quoted sums are requested as advance payments for renting a place. The period of renting can vary from three months to one year.

less evident. Therefore, the market entry barriers for organised crime are far greater than most general crimes, and operations require close cooperation between offenders (van Koppen 2013). Cross-border trafficking of human beings often involves complex processes of coordination, whereby finding suitable co-offenders requires building of sufficient trust. Therefore, organised crime offenders in human trafficking use social ties and networks to establish trust before any cooperation and collusion takes place (van Koppen 2013; Von Lampe & Johansen 2004). Social relations and network dynamics ensure that the recruitment of new offenders and the creation of new partnerships are not the same as traditional models claim. Family, friends and acquaintances work together and introduce each other to others and are the base of criminal entrepreneurship and expansion (Kleemans & Van de Bunt 1999).

The observed differences in the source of initial capital appear to be contingent on the type of market entry, i.e. independently or through an already established network or criminal organization, as well as on the type of market segment—outdoor, indoor and high-end. Independent traffickers may need to raise initial capital to secure access to clients (e.g. place on the street or in a brothel, window in a red light district, etc.), logistics (e.g. transportation, lodging, work permit, etc.) and visual make-over of the trafficked person, e.g. high-end clothing, accessories, cosmetics, hair and body care, etc. Some of them initially start in Bulgaria and re-invest the generated proceeds to fund cross-border trafficking (BG-E4).

Criminal entrepreneurs joining established trafficking networks or organisations do not need to cover all these cost by themselves, since the network or the group grants the access to these assets or at least they may receive initial capital for related expenses through the network or from the boss of the group. The investment is then repaid from the sex worker's earnings (BG-C10, BG-C1). Nevertheless, joining an established network requires the newcomers to prove they are trustworthy and accountable. This is also indicative that market entry for prostituting girls and women is also heavily contingent of social connections and networks. Among the possible sources of start-up capital mentioned by the interviewed respondents were borrowing money from friends, family and relatives (BG-C11, BG-C12, BG-C13, BG-E1); revenues from legal business (BG-C10), proceeds from another illegal activity (BG-C16, BG-E14) and loans from usurers (BG-C7).

Joining an established trafficking/procuring operation provides a number of advantages for both sex workers and pimps. Networks and groups have more available capital which can be channelled to serve different purposes as needed, such as recruitment activities, transport and accommodation abroad, as well as connections and a line of credit in case of urgencies. The advantage is most noticeable with regard to recruitment and starting costs. Apart from everything, starting an independent operation entails a number of risks. Independent sex workers are vulnerable to violent or fraudulent customers or to networks or groups trying to subdue them to their control. Procurers and traffickers not part of a group also have less resources and, therefore, have to carry out all activities associated with the business. Independent pimps and traffickers thus often choose to have or appear to have a limited number of sex workers under their control (up to 3) as with more women "the problems are bigger and are related to more costs" (BG-C20, BG-C11, BG-C12).

Borrowing money is also a tactic used to weather out difficult moments. However, borrowing from loan sharks is considered as highly risky due to the exorbitant interest rates and both pimps and sex workers try to avoid it. Generally, traffickers prefer to settle such situations through borrowing from other members of their network (BG-C3, BG-C13, BG-C20). Sex workers appear to have a broad creditor base, that includes pimps, colleagues and in some cases clients (BG-C16, BG-C23). There is a general arrangement that there are loan options for persons in the trafficking business with more favourable interest rates than those of loan sharks. The interest rates for such intra-industry/network lending are 10–20% (BG-C5, BG-C6, BG-C8). Rates may still be higher in cases of a novice who is yet to prove trustworthy.

1.4.2 Settlement of Payments

Data indicates that there are various modes for the settlement of payments within the trafficking network and outside actors alike, wherein the sole common denominator is the pre-eminence of cash transactions. Almost all payments are made in cash—clients pay cash to sex workers (variably before or after the service) and the money is subsequently transferred to the higher levels of the organisation in cash as well (BG-C1, BG-C10). Women report and account for their earnings to pimps "day by day" (BG-C6, BG-E19, BG-C4), often via coded messages through messaging services or SMS (BG-E17). Sex workers may receive their shares periodically in cash by their traffickers/procurers or trusted persons, in some cases every three days (BG-C3). Cash proceeds are then often transferred up the chain through trusted payment facilitators, which appear to be insiders rather than the typical money mule (BG-C10). Exceptions do exist as sometimes clients can pay for sexual services via bank transfer/credit card, whereby such payments are registered as a legitimate service, e.g. massage. This is particularly the case whereby trusted clients based in western European states order sex services from sex workers that may be currently based in Bulgaria. The wired money is used for travel and advance payment for the sexual services (BG-C5, BG-C16).

It should also be noted that in the domestic indoor and high-end prostitution segment, many sex workers have also fictitious contracts as office assistants, masseuses, waitresses, hostesses, barmaids, exotic dancers, receptionists, hotel maids, etc. The contracts are usually signed with bogus companies and fixed at minimum wage and for minimum working hours. However, they will still receive payments under these contracts and all respective social and healthcare contributions will also be covered. Some respondents report that they receive these payments via bank transfers (BG-C4, BG-C9). In this way the traffickers try to conceal the true nature of their activities and not raise suspicion in the law enforcement and other regulatory agencies (BG-E3, BG-E9).

Procurers and traffickers transferring profits from abroad may use money transfer services, such as Western Union (BG-C1). However, they will take a number of precautions, such as using intermediaries (money mules) to withdraw the money and deliver the amounts to the intended recipients (BG-C10). Western Union is also a preferred method for sex workers, who send small sums to their families (BG-C7, BG-C8, BG-C9). Another method for sending money to Bulgaria is through van drivers servicing routes from Bulgaria to western Europe, some of which may be part of other—irrelevant to sex—trafficking and/or smuggling networks, e.g. cannabis from the Netherlands (BG-C7, BG-E1, BG-E8).

Procurers and traffickers may use trusted third parties for settling payments with facilitators outside of the networks such as club owners or corrupt police. There is at least one account that describes a more sophisticated system of settling transactions. In this case the trafficking ring-leader uses a multitude of bank accounts under his control, which are registered to dummy entities or shell companies in order to transfer payments to external actors. The dummy accounts are employed on a rotating basis so as to avoid suspicion (BG-C1). Cash mules are also used, particularly for international payment settlements (BG-C10).

When operating abroad some traffickers are wary of getting directly involved in all payment settlement activities, as being seen around sex workers and in particular known clubs and hotels may arouse suspicion. Therefore, in some cases settlements with clubs and hotels are delegated to the women who may transact directly with the owners of the establishments where sex services are performed (BG-C13). Settlements in the domestic market seem to be conducted in cash directly between the trafficker, or trusted person, and the owner of the club/hotel where sexual services are provided (BG-C1, BG-C20).

The high-end prostitution segment displays some subtle differences in the patterns of payment settlements. In many cases the pre-supposed exclusivity of sexual services performed by "models" and the parallel operation of the fashion agency as a cover business seem to keep a certain distance between the consumer and the sex worker, particularly in the financial flows. The contacts between the customers and the clients are usually handled by a central figure inside the agency—the so called "booker." The booker also often receives the payment directly or through trusted members of the network from the client. Therefore, in such cases the women would perform a pre-arranged and pre-paid service without coming into contact with money. Exceptions seem to be the case, wherein established and known clients are concerned and wherein sex workers are paid directly by the client (BG-E6).

1.4.3 Costs of Doing Business

Trafficking operations involve a variety of different costs at each stage of the process—recruitment, transportation and exploitation, wherein the last stage appears to be most cost demanding. Some of these costs are one-off and might be categorised as investment costs, whereas others are recurring and rather fall under the operational costs category. It should be noted that this classification is somewhat arbitrary, since the line between the two is blurred. The costs structure of trafficking operations varies depending on the modus operandi of the traffickers.

Recruitment of new sex workers in most cases entails an investment of both financial resources and time. Independent traffickers, family-based organisations and loose networks often employ the so called "lover-boy" method or similar strategies involving deceit and manipulation. This method includes courting, befriending and manipulating the potential victim by the recruiter into a relationship of trust (BG-C1, BG-C7, BG-C14). While traffickers often rationalise their actions as helping the women earn good money (BG-E11), different degrees of manipulation are involved. Aside from poverty, other vulnerability factors play an important role as well—dysfunctional family background, lack of experience with adult relationships, recent emotional trauma due to relationship break-ups, and periods of stay in orphanages or other institutions for disadvantaged young adults (BG-C1, BG-C2).

In some instances, the process of trust-building may last up to nine or more months, thereby the lover-boy incurs sustained additional expenses (BG-C14). Very often recruiters identify and pick good looking women from poor backgrounds who can easily be impressed with a luxury lifestyle. The related costs in this sense include expenditures for restaurants, vacations, clothes and other gifts (BG-C1, BG-C7, BG-C14). On the other hand, to take advantage of the lover-boy routine in recruitment, the recruiter may increase the chance for successful manipulation by displaying a luxurious lifestyle, which includes an expensive brand automobile, branded clothing and accessories, an expensive smart phone and well-maintained physique (BG-C10).

Hierarchically structured organisations usually pay to specialised members of the organisation to perform these activities or pay to external actors on fee-for-service base. Persons in charge of recruitment receive a specific sum per new recruit and a bonus if she does well. The sums reported were between €100 and €250 and the bonus amounted at €500 (BG-C1, BG-C2, BG-C4). The money invested in recruitment activities are considered as running costs for the business and are covered out of the generated revenue (BG-C1, BG-C2, BG-C3, BG-C5, BG-C6, BG-C8, BG-C10). Still, in some cases, sex workers can be "acquired" without any direct financial cost—such as coercing or manipulating an independent prostitute to work for the network (BG-C1, BG-C2, BG-C4) or in cases where women seek out such employment themselves.

A common expense that is closely related to the recruitment stage are the costs for make-over and personal care of the newly recruited victims. Collected data suggests that these sums range from around €500 to €1500, which is used for brand clothing, accessories, cosmetics and perfumery, among others (BG-C8, BG-C10, BG-C9, BG-C22, BG-C7). The sum varies, since it depends on the modus operandi of the traffickers. The outdoor segment is less demanding with regards to such expenses, whereas for the indoor and the high-end prostitution segments these expenses are integral. There are instances, wherein more expensive manipulations such as plastic surgery might be invested in for high-end sex workers (BG-C18).

Transportation costs, both domestically and abroad, apparently play a minor role for the operations of Bulgarian traffickers, since Bulgarian citizens are entitled to a visa–free travel in the EU and the costs of intra-community travel have significantly decreased with the advent of low-cost flights. At the domestic market, if the provision of the sex service necessitates transportation to another location, it is either covered by the sex worker, or the procurer or is paid by the client on top of the price for the session. Procurers might enter into specific arrangements with taxi drivers or might provide transportation themselves (BG-C17, BG-E3, BG-E6, BG-E10). Regarding the transportation costs in cross-border trafficking all interviewed respondents reported that these are usually covered by the traffickers.

The most substantial costs sustained by the traffickers are related to the exploitation stage. These costs include lodging, expenditures for client acquisition, monitoring and control of sex workers, protection, concealment of criminal activities, corruption, and facilitation of money laundering.

Client acquisition costs or in other words securing access to clients is one of the most significant costs for trafficking operations. Depending on the modus operandi these costs might include costs for acquiring access to a profitable location on the street, a window in a red light district or a place in a well-established adult club, brothel, and massage parlour. Online advertising costs and payments to taxi drivers, hotel porters or concierges for referring clients can also be generally put in this category.

Profitable locations in hotels, motels and clubs abroad and in Bulgaria are often controlled by hierarchically structured groups and access to these for other trafficking actors is usually granted upon certain fee paid in advance (BG-C1, BG-C4, BG-C19, BG-C20, BG-E17). Even if the location is not controlled by some organised crime group, traffickers and pimps have to pay the hotels, motels and various hospitality businesses in order to use their facilities for sexual services undisturbed (BG-C15, BG-C17, BG-C4). In some arrangements the fee is flat and irrespective of the prostitute's earnings (BG-C4), whereas in other cases, the hotel's owner or manager receives a fixed fee (in one of the cases €5 per client) for each client brought in the hotel (BG-C17).

Seasonal prostitution at hotels in resorts on the Black Sea coast seems to be characterised by strong competition, which drives prices up, while at the same time some hotel managers may require payment in advance for the prostitutes to work in a protected environment with access to clients. The fee for one prostitute to work in a Black Sea resort hotel may vary between €2500 and €3125 (or €125 per night for a beachfront hotel) per sex worker per month in advance (BG-C1, BG-C3). The closer the hotel is to the beachfront, the higher the fee (BG-C3). The fee for working in adult clubs is around €1125 per sex worker per month (BG-C6). Different payment modalities exist, depending on the arrangement. In some cases, traffickers are required to pay a fixed fee upfront. This might be entry fee which is followed by a monthly or weekly payments (BG-C4). Alternatively, the lump sum covers stay for a certain amount of time—e.g. on seasonal basis (BG-C19, BG-E3). The amount differs depending mainly on the location and reputation of the establishment. Hotels and clubs in top Bulgarian summer resorts have been reported to cost €2000–€3750 per month (BG-C1, BG-C3, BG-C4, BG-C7). Smaller Bulgarian hotels or motels which provide terrain by the hour for the outdoor segment of the prostitution market might charge as little as €2.5–€5 per service (BG-C12, BG-C17).

Securing access to profitable windows, brothels, massage parlours and similar establishments in the red light districts of western European cities, where prostitution is legal, also often entails payment of fees in advance. Some of the respondents indicated that in order to secure placement of a sex worker in such establishments traffickers have to pay a one-off fee of €2000–€3000 to an established broker who has been active in the business for a significant amount of time and possess the necessary social and business connections (BG-E17, BG-E6).

Another option for traffickers is to rent apartments or houses where the women can work, wherein costs vary depending on the location. According to one of the respondents, an apartment in Cologne, close to the red light district, rented for several girls to provide sexual services may cost around €550 per month (BG-C6). This option is more prevalent in the indoor and high-end prostitution segments, and may be used in both domestic and cross-border trafficking (BG-E3, BG-C6, BG-E6).

Finally, many trafficking organisations rely extensively on online advertising for solicitation of clients. Various websites, social platforms and online mobile applications are used to advertise the sex services. Online advertising may cost from nothing to a few euro per week, which is negligent compared to the fees for placement at brothels or similar sex venues. Thus, the sex worker can provide the sex services in any rented apartment, at the place of residence of the client or in any hotel. However, in high-end prostitution organisations, organisers may also invest in marketing their "models", i.e. increase their popularity, hence marketability, through investing in professional photo sessions, magazine covers appearances, fashion shows, beauty pageants, among others (BG-E6).

Other client acquisition costs may also include payments to external facilitators that refer clients. There is evidence that in a Bulgarian summer resort, a trafficking network would pay €15 per secured client to taxi drivers, hotel porters and casino workers (BG-E30).

Monitoring, supervision and control of sex workers are the other type of costs associated with the exploitation stage, although they are not always easily quantifiable. These costs are primarily related to the strict accounting of the clients served and the due collection of the pre-agreed portion of earnings from the sex workers. In more coercive arrangements the tasks for monitoring and control also involve preventing the victim to run away or turn to the authorities. Depending on the complexity of the trafficking operation, these tasks may be performed by the traffickers themselves or by other trusted persons. Independent traffickers and members of loose networks often carry out these tasks by themselves (BG-C10, BG-C13, BG-C17), although in loose networks members could help each other from time to time (BG-C13). In family-based organisations usually one of the family members is tasked with this (BG-C14). In other words, they do not directly incur financial costs for this, although they invest personal time.

Hierarchically structured organisations usually have trusted persons that are managing the day-to-day schedule of the women, as well as the daily collection of the earnings. Use of such supervisors and money collectors also serves the purpose to conceal the direct link between the sex workers and the organisers of the trafficking operation. In Bulgaria the money that has been earned by the women is usually collected in cash daily by the persons in charge of protection and transportation of women (BG-C1, BG-C2, BG-C3, BG-C4, BG-C6, BG-C8, BG-C9, BG-C10, BG-C20). In the high-end prostitution segment, these tasks were carried out by the bookers, who are handling the contacts between the women and the customers (BG-E6). Different modus operandi is used by Bulgarian traffickers in western Europe, where this role is often assigned to some of the trusted sex workers (the so called "first girl"), the managers of the sex establishment where the victims are placed or the "madams" at the windows at red light districts in Belgium and the Netherlands (BG-C5, BG-C18, BG-C21, BG-C22, BG-C23, BG-E29). The amount of these costs remains somewhat unclear, although some of the respondents reported that the supervisors are paid a pre-agreed proportion from the earnings of the sex workers they look after (BG-E6, BG-C3, BG-C5).

Closely related to monitoring and control are the costs for protection of sex workers. Independent traffickers and family-based groups personally take care of the safety of the women and their earnings from abusive clients and rival competition (BG-C17). However, especially in the outdoor segment they are often subjected to protection racket by larger organised crime groups specialised in the use of violence (BG-12, BG-C14) and one of the interviewed offenders reported that he pays about €8 per night (or €60–€65 monthly) for each of his six workers working on the street (BG-C17).

Similarly, members in loose networks are responsible for the sex works they control but cooperate when they have to deal with rival competition. Rather rare are occasions, when they pay for protection to external persons (BG-C4). It should also be noted that, when traffickers pay for placement of their sex workers at brothels or other sex venues, the protection is included in the price or at least part of the pre-agreed arrangements. Hierarchically structured groups usually have members assigned with such tasks and, as mentioned above, they are often also responsible also for monitoring and control of women, money collection and transportation. Reportedly in such arrangements for every five to six sex workers there are two persons performing the day-to-day management, coordination, supervision and money collection (BG-C1, BG-C2). Most of the hierarchical groups also seem to retain within their ranks the so called "punitive brigades" that are part of the operating group and on the monthly payroll and are specialise in use of violence (BG-C7, BG-C10; BG-C18, BG-C19).

Corruption costs also generally fall into the category of cost of protection. Different trafficking actors make use of corruption to different degrees, corresponding to their specific needs. Corruption payments become much more necessary in cases of incidents, complaints by family members and initiation of investigations by the police and judicial authorities. Such payments are made either directly or through the help of intermediaries. Typical targets of corruption are law enforcement officers and to a lesser extent judicial authorities (Bezlov et al. 2016). Many respondents reported regular extortion fees imposed by police officers to outdoor and indoor sex workers and their procurers in Bulgaria (BG-C12, BG-C15, BG-C16, BG-C17, BG-C19).

Hierarchically structured groups sustaining more sophisticated trafficking operations incur additional costs related to the concealment of their activities from the authorities. In the high-end prostitution segment such costs may include investing in elaborate schemes of legitimate business structures—appointment of straw persons for owners and managers, registering front businesses such modelling or fashion agencies, and organizing model castings, fashion shows, advertising campaigns, among others (BG-E6). However, use of legitimate business structures is not limited to this segment. Criminal groups, which invest in and control adult clubs, massage parlours and similar establishments employ similar methods and register bogus companies with straw persons appearing as owners and managers. Women working in such adult clubs, hotels and other establishments have labour contracts as dancers, masseuses, office assistants or housekeepers (BG-C1, BG-C5, BG-C9). Using such legitimate companies as a front also entails a number of other costs typical for all normal legitimate businesses—office rents, accounting and legal services, utilities, staff salaries, etc. In recent years, trafficking networks that have established a foothold abroad also exhibit trends of attempting to use legitimate business structures through renting or investing in bars, clubs, restaurants and sex establishments in various western European cities (BG-E16, BG-17, BG-E19).

1.4.4 Profits and Profit Sharing

As with the costs for doing business, the revenues from trafficking operations vary depending on the modus operandi of the traffickers and the market segment in which they operate. Prices for sex services fluctuate from one market segment to the other, as well as on the domestic prostitution market and abroad. Sex workers in the different market segments also tend to handle different number of customers. Furthermore, the profit sharing arrangements between the traffickers and the sex workers also vary depending on the modus operandi.

The prices in the domestic market are significantly lower compared to the prices abroad. The sex workers in the domestic outdoor segment, which work on the street or bring their clients in low-end motels or hostels, charge between €7 and €15 depending on the service (BG-C12, BG-C17). Services in the indoor segment performed in clubs, hotels, rented apartments and private residences cost between €50 and €200. In summer and winter resorts the prices might go up to €200 per session. The high-end prostitution segment, which includes women procured to rich clients by model agencies can range from €300 to €500 (BG-E6), depending on the length of sessions (e.g. 2–4 h, overnight stay or weekend). Abroad, the prices vary in the different countries (e.g. prices in Greece are lower than prices in Germany) and depending on the location (e.g. window prostitution vs. call girl services). The prices in the outdoor segment are €30–€50 per session depending on the type of services provided (BG-C7, BG-C23). The prices in the indoor segment fluctuate significantly—from €50-€100 per hour for low-end motels or hotels (BG-C1, BG-C4, BG-C11, BG-C16, BG-C22) to €150–€400 for red light district windows, rented apartments and well-placed hotels (BG-E6, BG-C6, BG-C7, BG-C8). Prices of high-end sex workers abroad start from €400 up to €3000 but they also have longer engagements—e.g. over-night stay, weekend, etc. (BG-C9, BG-C18). Regular customers can receive discounts on sex services, usually about 5% (BG-C5, BG-C9).

Sex workers in different market segments also handle different number of clients. Whereas a sex worker in the outdoor segment will handle 7–20 clients per day (BG-C7, BG-C8), clients in the indoor segment are usually between two and six men per day (BG-C4, BG-C6, BG-C7, BG-C20). High-end escorts work with between one and six clients per week (BG-E6, BG-C9, BG-C18). The women usually work five-six days per week (BG-C16, BG-C19, BG-C23). The number of clients fluctuates from sex worker to sex worker but also depends on a number of other factors—location, day of the week, season; therefore, traffickers are constantly looking for more profitable locations or better performing sex workers. Nevertheless, according to the accounts of several interviewed traffickers operating in the indoor segment abroad, the average monthly revenue from a sex worker is in the range of €15,000–€45,000 (BG-E8, BG-C1, BG-C3, BG-C4, BG-C7, BG-C9).

Revenue sharing arrangements differ depending on the type of the trafficking organisation and the modus operandi of the traffickers. Independent traffickers and family based groups more often tend to withhold all earnings from the sex workers under different pretexts—either because the trafficker and the victim have some kind of intimate relation and he pretends to look after the "family money," or because the traffickers pretend to collect and safeguard the money on behalf of the victim until she returns to Bulgaria (BG-C14, BG-C15, BG-C21, BG-C22, BG-C23). In many of these cases deception, manipulation, coercion and even physical violence against the victim are also used by the traffickers. The procurer in this case will cover all costs of the trafficking operation from the earnings of the sex workers and keep the profit for himself.

Hierarchical groups and loose networks as a rule employ less often coercive methods and pre-negotiate the split of the revenues with the sex workers. The interviewed respondents reported different proportions of earnings, which the sex workers are allowed to keep. The share of earnings remaining in the sex workers oscillated between 20 and 50%. Most respondents report that the traffickers are supposed to cover all related expenses from their share—acquisition of clients, protection and monitoring, transport and lodging. In general, gifts and tips received by the sex workers are usually kept by them (BG-C4, BG-C6, BG-C8). Sex workers who generate more revenue can also be rewarded with a bonus by the traffickers—either with an increase in the share of earnings they are allowed to keep (although this never goes above 50%), or other perks such as an extra holiday (BG-C9). In some of the hierarchically structured organisations, some of the key members of the group are also allowed to receive a share of the revenues generated by the sex workers. For example, in one of the cases involving a modelling agency used as a cover for prostitution, the person who handled the contacts between the women and the customers received 10% of all earnings (BG-E6). Another respondent reported that as a supervisor of six sex workers, he was receiving 20% of their earnings (BG-C3).

Hierarchically structured organisations, which controlled brothels or other sex venues (especially such in a profitable location), follow a different arrangement for profit sharing. Instead of pre-agreeing on the split of the earnings, they demand a fixed advanced payment. For example, organisations controlling erotic clubs at Sunny Beach resort in Bulgaria demanded an advanced payment of €7500 per sex worker for three months during the summer season (BG-E3, BG-C20). Similar arrangements based on advanced payments ranging from €2500 to €7000 on a monthly basis were reported about hotels, adult clubs in other resort areas and abroad (BG-C1, BG-C2, BG-C3, BG-E6, BG-E17). The advanced payments supposedly cover their costs for renting the venue, providing protection against violent clients, rival groups and state authorities. The beneficial owners of such well-located adult clubs at the Bulgarian sea coast reportedly receive about €30,000 on a monthly basis in the form of rent (BG-E3).

The enforcement of the revenue sharing arrangements are very strict and traffickers often impose tight daily accounting and control. For example, when the appointments with clients are made through the internet, the persons in charge of protection and revenue collection are granted access to the profiles of the women and sometimes communicate with the customers directly (BG-C1, BG-C2, BG-C3, BG-C5, BG-C8). In other arrangements, sex workers have supervisors who closely account for their clients and earnings on a daily basis. Women who are caught trying to hide revenue are penalised with working for a certain amount of time without receiving any compensation (BG-C1, BG-C3, BG-C5, BG-C20). In rare cases they might be subject to physical violence, although it appears that this method is generally avoided, as well as the withholding of all earnings of the women. One trafficker, who used to be part of a larger network, notes: "There should be control but never through violence. I have always managed through conversations, good treatment and money, 50/50, always. If the girl wants, she can let you have all the money, but it is advisable to go 50/50" (BG-C10). The use of violence might prompt sex workers to go to the authorities (BG-C22).

The methods for money laundering and the re-investment of proceeds from human trafficking are rarely sophisticated, especially in the case of independent traffickers and loose networks. Moreover, much of the money is spent on a lavish lifestyle or supporting a drug habit. Money is returned to the country and laundered through the purchase of designer clothing, electronics and automobiles, often of luxury brands (BG-E10, BG-E13, BG-E14). The traffickers operating in the outdoor and low-priced indoor segments of the prostitution market and more independent traffickers appear also to be drawn to use of simple trade-base money laundering such as purchasing and re-selling of easily tradable goods. These include mostly cars and gold, which are brought in and sold in Bulgaria (BG-C7, BG-C10, BG-C11, BG-C12, BG-C13, BG-C15). Other consumer goods, e.g. stolen electronics, are also bought cheaply and subsequently resold (BG-C7). Purchasing real estate and land in Bulgaria remains popular both for traffickers and sex workers, and most of the interviewed offenders and sex workers reported such.

Traffickers who are part of more sophisticated organisations reportedly invest more often in various commercial establishments such as restaurants, small shops, hair salons (BG-C1, BG-C6, BG-C11). Investments into legitimate enterprises can serve a number of purposes—laundering of proceeds, providing a legitimate reason for residing abroad, recruitment of new sex workers—e.g. hair salons and massage parlours (BG-C1, BG-C10). Value transfers in the form of multiple donations and/or re-sales through a ring of dummy recipients are also reported to be employed in laundering proceeds from trafficking (BG-C10). Organisers in hierarchically structured groups, on the other hand, engage in developing more sophisticated and diversified legitimate business portfolios with multiple stakes in sectors such as hospitality, construction, agriculture, jewellery trade, fitness gyms, etc. (BG-C1, BG-C3, BG-C9). Construction works in and around popular winter and summer resorts as well as larger cities is a widely used method of laundering (BG-C6, BG-C16).

Generally, most of the proceeds are invested and laundered in Bulgaria but a tendency to invest abroad is beginning to be discerned (BG-E5). Previous research showed that in the first half of the 2010s there had been many instances of investment in real estate in Greece, Cyprus, Spain, Italy, and Germany (Bezlov et al. 2016). There are strong indications of a positive relationship between the sophistication of an OCG and its propensity to invest in real estate and businesses abroad, both as cover and investment for trafficking sustainability and expansion. These may include bars, clubs, and cafes, used often for criminal social networking and/or provision of sexual services (BG-E5, BG-E6, BG-E7, BG-E17, BG-E19). Some experts opined that there is development of a similar trend among independent traffickers as well (BG-E8).

1.5 The Role and Impact of the Internet on Human Trafficking Activities and Its Finances

The extensive penetration of internet-based services such as (anonymised) instant messaging and social networking websites has impacted on sex trafficking in Bulgaria and abroad in a variety of ways. First of all, online advertising has created opportunities to lower costs for client acquisition, since it reduced the competitive advantage of having access to established and profitable locations. Thus, especially in Sofia and abroad, it effectively contributed to the gradual disintegration of the existing cartelisation and control of the sex service market by organised crime and the increasing share of independent procurers and sex workers (CSD 2012). Furthermore, it also allowed expanding the pool of potential new recruits, since it provided a whole new bundle of opportunities to target and reach out to potential victims (CSD 2017). However, internet has also increased the risk for independent traffickers and sex workers, since they can be easily traced and eventually targeted by hierarchically structured groups, other rival competitors or law enforcement authorities. The latter is especially true for cities with relatively small prostitution markets (BG-C1, BG-C4, BG-C8).

Data from the interviews suggests that the reliance on and use of the internet for sex trafficking, including recruiting and customer base development, is anchored in the interplay of assessments for trustworthiness, opportunism and caution of exposure. For example, whereas the internet may present countless opportunities for recruitment and clientele expansion it is void of the typical offline mechanisms for establishing trust. This is why, it is not surprising that both traffickers and sex workers among interviewed respondents exhibit diverse attitudes toward the online environment depending on subjective preferences and risk perceptions, as well as experiences with rival competitors and law enforcement encounters (BG-C10, BG-C13). Utilisation of online services such as dating sites, social media and specialised websites differs greatly among the respondents, whereby both extremes of the spectrum are involved, e.g. no use versus exclusive use. Apparently, for some operations the internet proves sufficiently valuable so as to expand the network by including external facilitators, such as IT experts, thereby ensuring that the traffickers are able to fully enjoy the benefits and minimise the risks of internet exposure.

Internet services are primarily used for client acquisition and interviewed respondents provided a variety of examples how they are utilised. Many independent traffickers and sex workers rely on various online channels to market their services and solicit clients. One of the respondents reported extensive use of social networks to expand clientele, although new clients were usually accepted upon prior reference by already known clients (BG-C16). Data suggests that social media accounts (usually with fake names) are used for customer solicitation, whereby sex workers engage in maintaining flirtatious communication with their clients (BG-C16, BG-E10). At least one account shows that sex workers may organise themselves into Facebook groups, wherein sexual services are negotiated and arranged with customers within the social media service (BG-C17). There are also reports that Facebook pages are being created where girls advertise their legal front business, such as massage services (BG-C5, BG-E10). In online offering and negotiating of sexual services the details of the transaction are usually carried out through a conversation over Skype or anther medium which allows the customer to be seen and assessed for reliability (BG-C2, BG-C4).

Organised trafficking and prostitution networks also tend to use the internet for client acquisition, as well as for sex worker supervision and control. Victims may be instructed to register accounts and profiles on online dating sites that are popular in the country where they work, such as Badoo, eLove Dates, Tinder (for western Europe) and Gepime, Elmaz, Adam and Eva (for Bulgaria) (BG-C8, BG-C2, BG-C1). The accounts are controlled by the traffickers, whereby in some instances the organiser will hire an expert to deal with the technical details of account management, including for profiles in social media such as Facebook (BG-C8, BG-C6, BG-C1, BG-C5). Such experts are usually external to the network and are not involved on a full-time basis (BG-C5). The control and supervision activities include operating with the sex workers' accounts, messaging on their behalf, instructions not to delete chat messages with clients, regular inspection of the contents of chats, among others (BG-C8, BG-C1, BG-C3). Thus, apart from everything, ICT technologies have also reduced costs for supervision and control.

Hierarchical organisations, are also known to take advantage of internet to trace and recruit independent sex workers who use online dating sites to increase their exposure and popularity. The recruiters would regularly scan the known websites used for offering incognito sexual services and identify potential new recruits to be convinced to join the network. Once a victim is identified then the typical recruitment tactics of manipulation and coercion will ensue (BG-C1, BG-C4). Some of the interviewees were of the opinion that independent offering of sexual service through online dating and other sites is a short-term experience lasting up to several months. Then the independent sex worker is usually spotted by some local criminal group or network and they will instantly make efforts to recruit her/him (BG-C8, BG-C3).

This is why, a large group of traffickers and sex workers are cautious about using the internet actively for their operations because of uncontrollable exposure to the public, including rival competitors and law enforcement, and the perceived benefits of their own proven offline business model. Therefore, many consider face-to-face arrangements and negotiations to be more trusted, safe and reliable than internet-based communications, and therefore avoid online activities as a part of their risk-aversion strategy (BG-C10, BG-C12, BG-C13, BG-C14, BG-C15, BG-C21, BG-C22, BG-C23).

1.6 Conclusion

Human trafficking remains one of the most important sources of revenues for the Bulgarian organised crime. Although in the last decade the market has fragmented and decentralised, and the share of the independent traffickers and sex workers increased, it still remains largely controlled by organised crime. However, the modus operandi of all trafficking actors has shifted away from the violence and coercion towards the use of subtler methods involving economic incentives. The extensive penetration of the ICT and the steady growth of internet use have played an important role for these recent developments. Among other things, they have contributed to a significant reduction of client acquisition cost for trafficking operations.

The current analysis examined in-depth the financial underpinnings of the human trafficking both at the domestic market and abroad. There is a widely shared belief that human trafficking is practically low-cost criminal activity bringing huge profits, wherein market entry does not require any particular investment. The collected information to a large degree refutes this common myth at least in the Bulgarian context. Certainly recruitment and transportation costs can be negligent to none, but the exploitation stage does require initial investment, especially if it is expected to generate sufficient revenue. A big competitive advantage of Bulgarian traffickers is that being EU citizens they can enjoy visa free travel and low-cost transportation. However, client acquisition costs can be substantial, particularly for access to high profitable locations such as placement in an adult club at the sea coast resorts. Internet does provide an alternative and can significantly lower costs for client acquisition, but on the other hand it raises risks related to encountering abusive clients or coming across with rival competitors or extortionists. Thus, it also increases cost for protection. Expanding business is also related to additional costs for monitoring and controlling a larger number of sex workers, as well as costs for concealment of criminal activities, for example through establishing legitimate businesses as a cover. Nevertheless, the collected data indicates that social capital can alleviate or significantly reduce many of these costs for new-starters or provide them with the needed credit line to enter the business.

The extensive penetration of ICT services in prostitution markets have not changed much with regard to settlement of payments. Cash transactions still dominate trafficking business, whereas both payments from clients and within trafficking groups or networks remain in cash. The character of the money flows to a large extent predetermines the low sophistication of money laundering methods used by traffickers—money is moved across borders via non-bank money transfers and recently more often via money couriers. Subsequently the money is invested in real estate and cash-intensive businesses. Trade-based money laundering is also commonly used. The analysis also shows a newly emerged trend of criminal entrepreneurs investing their proceeds in the destination countries, especially in assets that allow them to expand their business—brothels or various hospitality businesses that are used as a cover for provision of sex services (e.g. restaurants, cafes, hotels, etc.).

References

Bezlov, T., Yordanova, M., & Stoynova, N. (2016). *Corruption and trafficking in women. The case of Bulgaria*. Sofia: Center for the Study of Democracy.

BKA. (2016). *Trafficking in human beings. National situation report 2015*. Wiesbaden.

CSD. (2007). *Organised crime in Bulgaria: Market and trends*. Sofia: Center for the Study of Democracy.

CSD. (2012). *Serious and organised crime threat assessment 2010–2011*. Sofia: Center for the Study of Democracy.

CSD. (2017). *Improving and sharing knowledge on the Internet role in the processes of human trafficking and smuggling*. Sofia: Center for the Study of Democracy.

CSD. (2018). *Serious and organised crime threat assessment 2012–2017*. Sofia: Center for the Study of Democracy.

Стойчев, С. (2016). *Проституцията в България: заплахи за човешката сигурност*. София: Институт за регионални и международни изследвания.

Europol. (2016). *Situation report. Trafficking in human beings in the EU*. The Hague.

GRETA. (2016). *Report concerning the implementation of the council of Europe convention on action against trafficking in human beings by Bulgaria*. Strasbourg.

ПРБ. (2010). *Доклад за прилагането на закона и дейността на прокуратурата и разследващите органи през 2009 г.*

ПРБ. (2013). *Доклад за прилагането на закона и дейността на прокуратурата и разследващите органи през 2012 г.* София.

ПРБ. (2017). *Доклад за прилагането на закона и дейността на прокуратурата и разследващите органи през 2016 г.* София.

ПРБ. (2018). *Доклад за прилагането на закона и дейността на прокуратурата и разследващите органи през 2017 г.* София.

Kleemans, E., & Van de Bunt, H. (1999). The social embeddedness of organised crime. *Transnational Organized Crime, 5*(January), 19–36.

Nationaal Rapporteur. (2017). *Slachtoffermonitor mensenhandel: 2012–2016*. Den Haag.

Риск Монитор. (2010). *Проституция и сексуална експлоатация*. София.

Petrunov, G. (2014). Human Trafficking in Eastern Europe: The case of Bulgaria. *Annals of the American Academy of Political and Social Science, 653*(1), 162–182.

van Koppen, M. V. (2013). Involvement mechanisms for organized crime. *Crime, Law and Social Change, 59*(1), 1–20.

Von Lampe, K., & Johansen, P. O. (2004). Organized crime and trust: On the conceptualization and empirical relevance of trust in the context of criminal networks. *Global Crime, 6*(2), 159–184.

Chapter 2
Human Trafficking and Its Financial Management in Italy

2.1 Introduction

Italy represents a southern European criminal hub and a destination and transit country for migrants arriving from North and West Africa, Eastern Europe, the Balkans and China (Shelley 2014) with most of the individuals arriving from Libya. After the bilateral agreement between Libya and Italy in 2009 as to jointly prevent irregular migration, the collapse of Qaddafi regime in 2011 and the related security vacuum, migration flows through the Central Mediterranean route have increased (IT-E5; IT-E7; IT-E15). Recent data from IOM (2018a), report a total of 119,310 arrivals by sea to Italy in 2017 and a total of 181,436 in 2016. Some estimations on the number of migrants that are further trafficked in Italy are available; however, the covert nature of this criminal market and the lack of centralised database do not allow for updated and comprehensive estimations and monitoring (Eurostat 2015). Trafficking in human beings for sexual and labour exploitation in Italy is mainly managed by foreign OCGs. Although their *modi operandi* have been largely documented (Cabras 2015; Ministero dell'Interno 2015; Save the Children 2017; Mancuso 2013; Campana and Varese 2015; Baldoni 2011; Carchedi 2010; Curtol et al. 2004; Sagnet and Palmisano 2015; Leogrande 2016; Palmisano 2017; Scotto 2016; Iovino 2016), little is still known on how these groups raise and manage capitals to finance and sustain their trafficking operations. The present chapter provides an account of the financial management of trafficking in human beings in Italy.

2.2 Market Overview

The prevalence of migrants arriving to Italy from Africa is due to the key role of the Central Mediterranean route. Data from FRONTEX (2017) underline that since 2014 the number of detections of illegal migrants crossing the Central Mediterranean Sea has exceeded 100,000. This is related to the persistent pressure of arrivals of migrants

G. A. Antonopoulos et al., *Human Trafficking Finances*, SpringerBriefs in Criminology, https://doi.org/10.1007/978-3-030-17809-3_2

from Libya, which is the main departure country into Europe, and whose social and political instability has favoured both trafficking and smuggling of human beings (Wittenberg 2017). Notwithstanding this, FRONTEX (2018) reports a drop in the illegal border-crossings using the Central Mediterranean route between 2016 and 2017. If on one side the trend of an increasing number of irregular migrants detected at the EU borders has characterised 2016 and a part of 2017, on the other it is in July 2017 that "*the numbers dropped suddenly and markedly to less than a half the level of June and July [2016] followed by an even larger fall to almost a third of that level in August [2017]*" (FRONTEX 2018: 18). Consistently, data from IOM (2018b) reports a decrease in the number of arrivals of migrants to Europe from 2016 to 2017, with estimated numbers of 390,432 and 186,768, respectively. In particular, in the period between January and November 2018, Italy has registered a total of 23,011 migrants arriving by sea corresponding to an 80% drop compared to the same period in 2017 (117,042 arrivals). A decrease (88%) is registered also for arrivals from Libya, representing around 56% of all the departures of migrants reaching Italy. Other countries of departures were Tunisia, Turkey and to a lesser extent Algeria and Greece. According to the data provided by the Ministry of the Interior (MOI) for the same period, Tunisia is the first declared country of origin (5002 arrivals, 22% of the total) followed by Eritrea (14%), Iraq, Sudan and Pakistan (7%) and Nigeria (5%), (IOM 2018c). Several factors are responsible for this trend. Firstly, internal transformations in Libya that in the second part of 2017 prevented departures of irregular migrants. Secondly, more migrants from Tunisia and Algeria embark with boats from their home countries and reach Sicily and Sardinia in Italy. Thirdly, the Turkey-Italy maritime route that has remained available to smugglers (FRONTEX 2018).

Although migration routes change over time as smugglers adapt to law enforcement counteraction and borders patrol, at present three main routes can be identified from Africa to Italy (major transit point) and then other European countries: (a) *Western route* for which the main source countries are Mali, Gambia and Senegal. This route usually connects in the Sahel with the Central route for which source countries are Nigeria, Ghana and Niger; (b) *Central route*, in which the country of major flow is Cameroon and that through Chad connects to the Western route in Niger (city of Madama) and further reaches Libya and the city of Sebha; (c) *Eastern route* for which source countries are mainly Somalia, Eritrea, Darfur in Sudan, and which usually cuts north through Sudan and Egypt and then along the coast of Africa (MEDU 2018; Reitano et al. 2014; Commissione Parlamentare di inchiesta sul fenomeno delle mafie e sulle altre associazioni criminali, anche straniere 2017) (Fig. 2.1).

All these routes converge to Maghreb, and in most recent years in Libya. "*In all the judicial cases, women and girls follow the sea route and cross almost the same stops. Here they are located in facilities, named differently 'connection houses' or 'ghetto houses', that are hell on earth. Warehouses for migrants where they suffer violence and deprivation*" (IT-E24). For example, Amnesty International (2015) has reported that since 2013, abductions of Sub-Saharan migrants and refugees for ransom along the different trafficking routes in Libya have increased. Migrants are handed over or

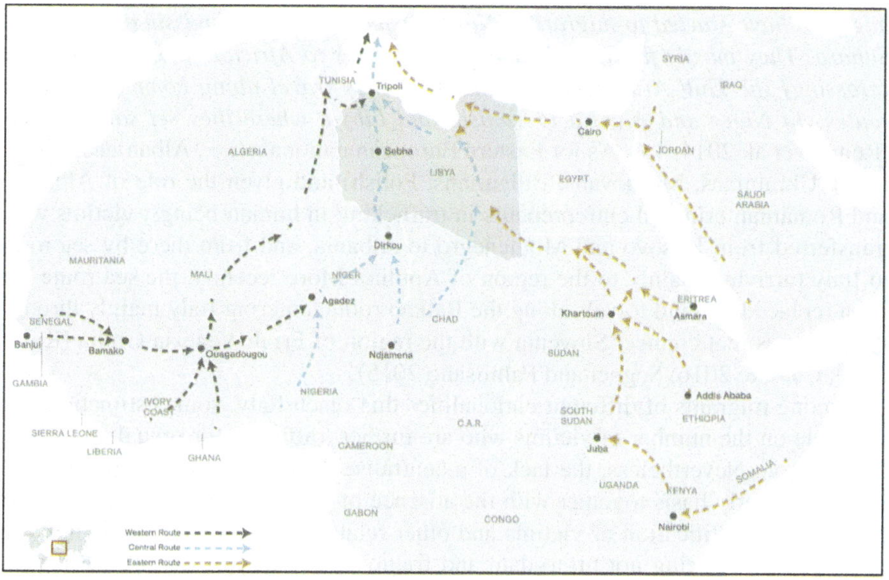

Fig. 2.1 Migratory routes from Sub-Saharan countries to Europe. *Source* Authors' elaboration on MSNBC (2018)

sold by traffickers to criminal groups upon crossing the border or arrival at major transit points, and then held like prisoners in private houses as well as subjected to torture and other ill-treatment for the purpose of extortion. These criminal groups are transnational and formed of nationals from Sub-Saharan African countries and Libyans. These abuses (e.g., being beaten, being subjected to electric shocks, insufficient food and water) have been documented in Sebha and its surroundings, as well as in transit points (e.g., Ajdabya, the main hub for migrants arriving from Somalia, Sudan, Eritrea and Ethiopia).

The majority of Chinese migrants in Italy originate from Zhejiang and Fujian provinces in the South of China, followed by Liaoning and Shandong provinces (North of China). Migrations from the North part of China that has started in more recent years, have been boosted by the expansion of the Southern area as a result of money remittances of migrants abroad (Beretta et al. 2016). Trafficked migrants arrive to Italy through different sea, air and land routes: Eastern Europe route, crossing Romania, Hungary, Albania, the Czech Republic and the former Yugoslavia; Western Europe route, passing through Austria, France, Germany and Malta before reaching Italy. Other used routes are from Albania, via the Strait of Otranto, to the port of Brindisi; or from Northern China, via the Maritime (Primor'ye) Territory of Russia, as to reach the city of Moscow where they get/buy visas to enter to Italy (Eastwest.eu 2013). "*I have seen different routes [for] China-Italy, passing through Turkey and Afghanistan, or other long land routes where illegal migrants were sold to different groups of traffickers*" (IT-E2). In more recent times, "*Asian and Indian migrants have started to migrate to North Africa overland by passing through the Sahara. They mostly fly from their home countries to African capitals sometimes [crossing] the Gulf Arab States. From there, they travel along common Saharan routes via Niger and Algeria to Tunisia and Libya, where they set sail to Italy*" (Reitano et al. 2014: 13). As for Eastern European nationals (i.e., Albanians, Romanians, Ukrainians, Moldovans, Bulgarians, Polish) and given the role of Albanian and Romanian criminal entrepreneurs in trafficking in human beings, victims were transferred from Kosovo and Montenegro to Albania, and from there by sea route to Italy (arriving mainly to the region of Apulia). More recently, the sea route has been replaced by land travels along the Balkan route, entering Italy mainly through the passages that connect Slovenia with the region of Friuli-Venezia Giulia (Russo 2010; Ciconte 2016; Sagnet and Palmisano 2015).

Among migrants of different nationalities that reach Italy, some estimations are available on the number of victims who are further trafficked for sexual and labour exploitation. Nevertheless, the lack of a centralised database and the collection of data on a yearly basis together with the absence of a uniform identification system render the quantification of victims and other related information (e.g. nationality, age, gender) as being not up-to-date and fragmented (GRETA 2016, 2019).[1] The Department of Equal Opportunities (DEO) gathers some data on the victims that have entered assistance, protection and social integration programmes funded by the same Department.[2] According to the last estimations available, in 2016 assisted victims totalled 1172, among which 81.4% were females (954), 17.6% were males (206), and 1.0% were transsexuals (12). The majority were adults (90.5%) ahead of 9.5% of underage victims. Most of the victims are exploited in the sex market (674 persons, 57.5%), but cases of forced labour were registered (92), forced criminality (37), forced begging (15), forced marriage (1), and multiple exploitation (72) (Department of Equal Opportunities 2018). In 2017, the number of assisted victims of trafficking was 1050 among which 85.6% were female and 11.5% were children. By the 16th of October 2018 (last data available) the number of assisted victims was 569, with 92.6% being females and 7.3% of children. Sexual exploitation counted for the highest percentage (90%), and in lower percentages labour exploitation (7%), forced begging (1.5%) and forced criminality (0.2%). In 2017 and 2018, the main countries of origins of trafficked victims were Nigeria, Romania, Morocco, Bangladesh, Pakistan, Albania and Bulgaria (GRETA 2019).

---

[1] As stated by GRETA (2019: 9), there is "*a significant gap between the [estimations provided] of assisted victims and the real scale of [...] human trafficking in Italy, due to difficulties in the detection and identification of victims [...], problems of data collection, and insufficient attention to trafficking for purposes other than sexual exploitation, as well as to internal trafficking. The authorities acknowledge that mixed migration flows make it difficult to distinguish between migrants and those who are trafficked and/or in need of international protection*".

[2] Through annual calls addressed to NGOs and non-profit organisations, the Department of Equal Opportunities grants funds for interventions of social protection under Art. 18 of Legislative Decree n. 286/1998 on "Consolidated text of provisions regulating migration and the rules relating the status of foreign nationals" and under Art. 13 of Law n. 228/09 on "Measures against trafficking in persons".

The International Organization for Migration (IOM) also provides data on potential victims of trafficking, that are interviewed from operators in the places of first arrival (ports and other hotspots) on the basis of a set of relevant indicators (e.g., age and sex, nationality, psycho-physical condition, level of education, family background, travelling mode, etc.). In 2016, a total of 8277 *potential* victims were identified; this compares with 6599 *ascertained* trafficked victims. A small part of the latter has been signalled and referred to the competent police and judicial authorities as well as to protection programs (IOM 2017).

There are recurrent reasons among migrants for leaving. The need for international protection or to escape from instability and violence, or living in poverty in the countries of origin. Thus, recruiters are facilitated by these factors. In Africa, for example, potential victims of very young age are approached in poor villages, and the same occurs in China and Eastern European countries such as Bulgaria, Romania, Albania, Ukraine, Poland, (IT-E7; IT-E22), (see IOM 2017; Politi and Fick 2015). In most cases, families play a crucial role during the recruitment stage (IT-E4; IT-E9; IT-E8; IT-E10): "*A family mandate, with recruiters that may be friends or country fellows of both sexes, although women are more suitable for this role since [they are] dressed well, and [are] looking wealthier*" (IT-E8). East European victims may be recruited by partners or presumed partners (i.e., the 'lover boy' method) as well.

The major trend seems to be that recruiters lure potential victims with the promise of legitimate well-paid jobs such as, for example, as hairdressers, caretakers, dancers, waitresses (IT-E10), and this can also occur on the Internet and social media such as Facebook. The general scheme displays as follows: "*the trafficker or the person linked to [OCGs] attract potential victims online. Among these [individuals] a virtual relationship is established based on dreams, false expectations and promises of a better future life; they plan weddings and travels and send presents or money to convince the [contacted person] to leave for Europe or Italy*" (Di Nicola et al. 2017: 50). E-recruitment is usually linked to the organisation of travels and specific Facebook pages where complete packages of service are offered (i.e., job offers, travel options, and documents) with reference to travels to Europe and Italy. "*Evidence from the investigation activity is the presence of Facebook profiles related to persons that offer travel arrangements and different options*" (IT-E19). Consistently "*our police officers... at ports have reported that some potential victims once arrived in Italy show to them the screenshot of a Facebook profile of the person that has organised their travel*" (IT-E15). An interviewed expert has also pointed out that besides direct recruiting, pages of Facebook where women and girls post pictures portraying them in nice situations (i.e., well-dressed, holding mobile phones, and having fun) serve as an attractive factor for others to leave their country (IT-E24). While communications between recruiters and traffickers is mainly through the digital mobile app WhatsApp as to avoid interceptions, the latter may be used to receiving pictures of potential victims that were previously contacted on Facebook. This is similar to the use of mobiles or emails by recruiters to send pictures of potential victims to exploiters (IT-E20; IT-E24). As for recruitment aimed at labour exploitation, both online and offline channels are employed, which include pages with online job advertisements and employment agencies (Leogrande 2016).

Migrants may travel with or without documents. In general, Nigerian victims who arrive by sea do not have passports, and once in Italy exploiters suggest to lodge asylum claims. "*The more recent trend, compared to recover victims as soon as possible, is to leave them in shelter centres and wait for the resident permit to be issued. Thus, it is safer when they are on the streets*" (IT-E24).[3] Travels by plane are also reported (even if at present they are less frequent) to the European airports using fake documents, as well as reaching Italy by train (IT-E18; IT-E20).

Similarly, Eastern Europeans (i.e., Albanians and Ukrainians), may be provided by traffickers with false documents, while the Chinese travel with touristic or study visas, obtained thanks to intermediaries in China. "*An additional service offered, facilitated by a corruptive mechanism. Under payment it is possible to obtain the documents needed*" (IT-E2). Another way, is through licensed tour operators which are granted blanket visas, and which seem to charge a fee for those that do not return after the expiration date. The trend seems to travel with genuine passports to depart the country, and then switch to forged or fraudulently obtained documentation (UNODC 2013). In Italy, documents are in most cases confiscated by exploiters, as to isolate the victims and make them more vulnerable (IT-E14; IT-E7), (see Leogrande 2016). In others, new fake documents are provided, as to be safe from police controls or to request resident permits. "*When migrants arrive to Lampedusa, they are subsequently directed to a specific neighbour of the city of Naples where, according to our intelligence, has emerged a high concentration of forgers. It does not seem a coincidence*" (IT-E10). The debt bondage, linked to travel and/or documents expenses as well as access to work, represents the main factor allowing traffickers to exploit victims within the sexual and labour markets in Italy, while using if necessary the treat of violent retaliation against family members if the victims are reluctant (IT-E2; IT-E10; IT-E14; IT-E21), (see Beretta et al. 2016; Eastwest.eu 2013; Commissione Parlamentare di inchiesta sul fenomeno delle mafie e sulle altre associazioni criminali, anche straniere 2017).

[3]Most migrants from Africa and travelling by sea are recovered in shelter centres, named "Centri di primo soccorso e accoglienza (CPSA)", where they receive first aid and are identified by law enforcement. These centres are located respectively in the cities of Agrigento and Lampedusa (Sicily); Cagliari and Elmas (Sardinia); Lecce and Otranto (Apulia); Ragusa and Pozzallo (Sicily). If the condition of 'asylum seeker' is recognised, migrants can obtain the residence permit to stay in Italy. In practice, their request is evaluated by a territorial commission that can either accept or refuse. In many cases, requests are refused and migrants have the right to appeal. In the meantime, and until the final decision of the commission is reached, they can remain in the national territory (IT-E15; IT-E24).

2.3 Market Structure and Social Organisation of Trafficking Networks

Foreign OCGs such as the Nigerians, Chinese and Eastern Europeans (i.e., Albanian, Romanian, Ukrainian, and Polish) are involved in the sexual and labour exploitative markets in Italy (DIA 2017; DNA 2017). Although settled throughout the country, it is possible to identify specific hubs for these two forms of exploitation: the cities of Turin, Milan in the North, Naples, Castel Volturno and Palermo in the South for sexual exploitation managed by Nigerian, Albanian and Romanian criminal entrepreneurs, and the province of Foggia with the area of Capitanata as a main point for labour exploitation in agriculture, especially for tomato harvesting (IT-E5; IT-E23; IT-E18), (see Scotto 2016).

These criminal entrepreneurs share similar organisational characteristics. They are small in size (ranging from 3–4 to 10–15 members) and are based on family, ethnic and tribal bonds, while operating within large fluid networks of individuals/groups made up of nodes present in both countries of origin and exploitation. These nodes are also connected to traffickers/smugglers (in the form of joint ventures) in transit countries as to facilitate the movement of victims. Although roles and duties tend to be related to hierarchy, personal skills and the location of individuals, in most cases they are interchangeable (IT-E9; IT-E6; IT-E2; IT-E18), (see DNA 2017; Becucci 2016; Carchedi 2016). The "*main feature of Chinese OCGs is that of guanxi, a term referred to a network of relationships among members on the basis of family bonds or commercial interests. These groups, that have mainly settled in the North and Centre of Italy, may create alliances to share duties and criminal markets, or may fight to control their territories*" (Eastwest.eu 2013: 102). Albanian and Romanian criminal entrepreneurs are structured into family-based groups. The members come from the same city or town, and groups are connected with the bosses that reside in the countries of origin and/or other small groups (i.e., cells). The latter usually manage the first stage of trafficking, being involved in recruiting victims and in organising their travel, also procuring documents if needed. They may also be in charge of intimidating the families of reluctant victims. More often, Albanian and Romanian OGCs collaborate in exploiting victims in the sex market, with the former controlling prostitutes on the streets (Ciconte 2016; Carchedi and Tola 2005). As stated by Palmisano (2017), in regard to trafficking for sexual exploitation, Albanians have been able to establish a high level position compared to other foreign OCGs in the North part of Italy, and the same occurs for the placement of forced victims in the construction industry. Ukrainians are active in the region of Campania and the city of Naples, and are structured into small-medium criminal groups with strong connections with bosses and groups in the country of origin. These criminal entrepreneurs may be more or less organised, and in some criminal proceedings have been defined as "*[mafia-type] associations, due to the systematic intimidations and retaliations for control purposes, illegal immigration and forced prostitution*" (Ingrascì 2016).

Nigerian Cults (named for example *Black Axe, Eiye, Aye, Buccaneers, Vikings, Ku Klux Klan Fraternity*), are small groups integrated within Nigerian OCGs.[4] Dated back to the 1980s, their members settled first in the Northern and Southern regions such as Piedmont (city of Turin), Campania (cities of Naples and Castel Volturno), and Sicily (cities of Palermo and Catania). At present, "*the power that these groups exercise in Italy is similar to that of Italian mafias. They manage drug trafficking, prostitution, and other criminal activities, and behave like our mafiosi in acquiring the control of local territories. In some criminal proceedings this characteristic has been recognised*" (IT-E22; IT-E21), (see DNA 2017; DIA 2017). In particular, the Cults support the *Maman* in managing criminal activities, and protect these businesses from other native competitors. The *Maman* is usually a previously exploited woman able to marry an Italian man or to obtain the residence permit, and is the point of connection between the 'bottom' and 'upper' parts of Nigerian OCGs in regard to sexual exploitation, i.e., members/individuals that produce profits and invest revenues in the legal economy (IT-E5, IT-E6; IT-E7; IT-E21; IT-E24), (see Ciconte 2016; Carchedi 2016). The structure of Nigerian OCGs and the roles of members in regard to trafficking and sexual exploitation is described as follows: "*Members in Nigeria are involved in the necessary stages to bring victims to Europe such as obtaining visas, hosting girls in accommodations while waiting for documents, managing voodoo rites (named juju) on girls to formalise the obligation to settle their debts, [and] arranging travels. The members active in Italy, cooperate to obtain and assure illegal entries of victims to Italy or Europe, to find Mamans that manage women and girls and their prostitution activity, to arrange accommodations, to gather profits and to intimidate victims*" (IT-E20).

Native organised crime groups (Cosa Nostra, the 'Ndrangheta, Camorra, and Sacra Corona Unita) are not directly involved in sexual and labour exploitation at the national level. The reason is the negative trade-off between profits and risks, compared for example to drug trafficking (IT-E14; IT-E15). Foreign OCGs are thus more or less independent in managing these illicit businesses (IT-E1; IT-E15; IT-E18) (see Leogrande 2016). In the territories where Italian OCGs are present, they had to reach agreements also consisting in the exchange of illegal services or goods (DIA 2017). "*If ten Polish men decide to be gangmasters in Cerignola [region of Apulia] they are not able to do anything without the support of local bosses. And if they have settled a human trafficking activity, they cannot avoid to have some relations with local organised crime groups*" (Leogrande 2016: 89). In Campania and Calabria, for example, Albanian OCGs exchange drugs at a favourable price with the consent to use areas of the local territories for sexual exploitation (IT-E8), (see Russo 2010). Similarly, along the Apulian, Calabrian and Sicilian coasts, foreign OCGs supply native OCGs with drugs, weapons, and contraband tobacco products while the latter

[4]From Italian judicial cases on the trafficking of Nigerian women and girls, cults inspired by Evangelical-Christian and animist beliefs are active both in Nigeria and within Nigerian communities in Italy. These cults behave like criminal organisations and recruit members through a strict selective process. Their role is to support Nigerian OCGs in protecting businesses, recovering debts, and settling disputes. In few cases, their involvement in physical mutilations against competitors and ritual homicides has been detected in Italy (IT-E9; IT-E15) (see Carchedi 2016).

offer support in logistics for the disembarkment of clandestine migrants and control to prevent law enforcement counteraction. In other cases, Italian OCGs have received monetary payments for each disembarkment of migrants or for the use of prostitution areas (Spiezia 2008).

2.3.1 Sexual Exploitation: The Central Role of Female Criminal Entrepreneurs

"*In the Italian sex market, there are Romanians, Albanians, followed by Nigerians and Chinese*" (IT-E10). When migrants (especially Nigerians) arrive in Italy, they have a mobile, also used by exploiters for remote control via global positioning system (GPS), and a telephone number to call to receive details as how to reach the final destination. Mobiles, in some cases, are also used to send bus or train tickets or if recharged to sell credits to other migrants and then pay for the journey. Potential victims, may be even picked up at shelter centres by members of OCGs or individuals recruited for this purpose (i.e., called ticket men), (IT-E4; IT-E8; IT-E21). "*Compared to the first migration flows where victims arrived with numbers written on papers and hidden in their hair, nowadays it is more likely that they call families in Nigeria that, in turn, inform exploiters of their arrival in Italy. It is a countermeasure of traffickers due to police controls when victims disembark*" (IT-E24). When victims start to be exploited, Nigerians work on the street and can be forced into prostitution at the very beginning inside or in the surroundings of open reception centres or temporary reception centres.[5] Eastern European and Chinese victims work mainly in closed places—i.e., apartments/massage centres, and the former approach at first clients in the streets or via the Internet (IT-E2; IT-E14; IT-E19). "*Exploiters buy telephone numbers connected in series that women and girls use to be contacted by clients, and that are linked to the offers of prostitution services posted on the Internet websites or social networks*" (IT-E10).

Common elements may be traced in the exploitation schemes applied by foreign OCGs. Firstly, the high level of internal trafficking or movement of victims. They are frequently moved from one city/town to another and usually work in places distant from where they live (IT-E20). "*At nights or early in the morning, regional trains from the city of Rimini to the city of Bologna are full of Nigerian women that travel for working reasons*" (IT-E10).

Secondly, the use of violence to force victims, especially reluctant ones, into prostitution. Nigerians, in particular, benefit from the use the voodoo rites (also called juju) celebrated by local 'holy men' in Nigeria before the departure of the victims as a guarantee of the contracted debt (IT-E18). In extreme situations, Nigerian traffickers resort to violence (IT-E19; IT-E20). The violent approach and treatment is typical for Eastern European OCGs (especially Albanians), as means of psychological sub-

[5]These places are respectively "Centri di accoglienza per richiedenti asilo—CARA" and "Centri di accoglienza straordinaria—CAS".

mission of victims and to enforce their loyalty. Nevertheless, since the 2000s, these criminal entrepreneurs have lowered the use of violence as a strategy to curb their business risk (Baldoni 2011). "*They are more contractual in leaving few hundred euros to the victims, and allowing more freedom in dressing and eating. During the '90s earnings for women and girls were equal to zero. More recently, a similar trend seems to involve Nigerian OCGs as well*" (IT-E8). Due to the intimidating force of the voodoo rite, Nigerian victims are not directly controlled when working; on the contrary the Eastern Europeans are subjected to strict supervision by members or employees of OCGs (IT-E18).

Thirdly, the central role of females in managing exploited victims, in most cases supported by their partners or other male/female assistants. The Nigerian *Maman*, who may also work as a prostitute (IT-E18; IT-E20), controls (i.e., demanding messages via mobile after each service) and organises trafficked victims, coordinates their activities and collects the income they make (IT-E19; IT-E24). Males (also partners) provide support through coercive and violent means when victims are reluctant or intend to emancipate (Baldoni 2011). In some cases, exploited victims live with the *Maman*, in others they are located in different apartments with other exploited women and girls, some of which may have legal residence permits as to be secured from police control (IT-E7; IT-E15; IT-E20). The *Maman* may be supported by male or female assistants and other members or recruited individuals, depending on the number of victims as shown in Table 2.1.

A study carried out in the city of Asti [region of Piedmont] has underlined that 3 or 4 *Maman* are active, each exploiting from 4 to 6 victims, and receiving the support of female assistants (named *Petit maman*) with different roles. One *Maman*, in a medium-high level position, is in relation with a partner belonging to a Cult and in charge of intimidations and debt recovery (Carchedi 2016). Similarly, Chinese prostitution is managed by females (i.e., arranging appointments, collecting profits, distributing money, providing food and clothes for the victims) who can be supported by males (IT-E14), (Beretta et al. 2016). Concurrently, Albanian women, after years of prostitution and similarly to Nigerian ones, can control small groups of 3–4 victims, supported by partners or other male members of OCGs (IT-E3), (see Russo 2010).

Table 2.1 Numbers of victims and corresponding units of criminal entrepreneurs in a local context

Victims	Maman	Partner	Handyman	Bodyguard	Supervisor	Cashier	Courier—Transporter from/to Nigeria
1–3	x						
4–6	x	x	x				
7–10	x	x	x	X			
11–15	x	x	x	X	x		
15+	x	x	x	X	x	x	x

Source Authors' elaboration on Carchedi (2016)

2.3.2 Labour Exploitation: The Key Role of the Agricultural Sector

The economic sectors of labour exploitation in Italy are the textile, construction, tourist and hotel industry, food service, and in particular agriculture (IT-E10; IT-E11), (Shelley 2014; Palmisano 2017). The exploitation of Nigerians as drug sellers has been reported, together with other occupations such as parking attendants, window washers and beggars regarding other nationalities. Female victims from Eastern Europe (e.g., Bulgarians, Romanians) are exploited as caregivers (IT-E12; IT-E4; IT-E6), (see Bertolotti 2017; Save the Children 2017).

Chinese migrants are mainly exploited in textile and clothing factories, or in restaurants, where employers may be either Chinese or Italians, who have transient relationships of reciprocal interest with traffickers. It is more likely that the owners of factories/companies (especially Chinese) know the criminal entrepreneurs involved in illegal immigration (i.e., named *shetou*) and rely on them to acquire labour force at low cost (IT-E2), (see Becucci 2016). The opposite may also occur. In one police investigation, the Chinese trafficker was in contact with two Italian representatives of a job placement cooperative, compliant in delivering fictitious contracts and fake paycheques (IT-E14). In other cases, there is no link between traffickers and employers, thus within the Chinese community, a recruitment service exists based on dedicated bars and newspapers, as for example in the city of Milan (Beretta et al. 2016).

East Europeans and Sub-Saharan Africans are the main groups exploited in the agricultural sector, with the highest concentration in the province of Foggia (i.e., the area of Capitanata) in the region of Apulia (Sagnet and Palmisano 2015; Ciconte and Liberti 2016). Nevertheless, migrants are subjected to constant internal exploitation from North to South due to the specificity of harvesting seasons (IT-E11; IT-E16), (see Leogrande 2016). "*By the end of winter they brought us to pick potatoes at Cassibile [in Sicily], then they told us we had to go to Apulia. It is four years that we make this travel. […] When we arrived to the city of Lecce, they brought us with a light van to an Algerian man, in the farmlands of the town of Nardò*" (Sagnet and Palmisano 2015: 19–20). This form of exploitation involves also Italians, especially as a result of the economic crisis, while in regard to migrants it is difficult to clearly distinguish between *trafficked* and *smuggled* individuals. "*It is hard to prove that the person employed in the tomato cultivation in Apulia is exploited as a consequence of trafficking. It is a multi-faceted situation. Migrants arrive through different illegal ways, and even if they have resident permits, they remain in a vulnerable situation. More likely, the discriminatory variable is the debt bondage. Slavery is the tip of the iceberg, under which there is just the exploitation of migrants*" (IT-E11). Both foreign and native OCGs benefit from what can be defined a "criminal system" in which legal and illegal entrepreneurs operate based on the ancient Italian labour method of gangmasters, that at present is functional to respond to and profit from the dynamics of the modern food industry (IT-E11; IT-E17), (see Scotto 2016).[6]

[6]The fact that farmers have to keep very low production costs depend on the dynamics of the globalised food market where their power to negotiate prices with industries that process their

Foreign OCGs may recruit individuals with the promise of a legal job, arrange their travel and their further employment in agriculture in slavery conditions, as in the case of Polish or Romanian OCGs (Iovino 2016; Leogrande 2016). For example, in the police operation "Piana" (from the location of farmlands, Piana del Sele), carried out in the province of Salerno, a transnational criminal organisation comprising of Romanians and Italians was dismantled after lawsuits from some of the Romanian victims. The offenders were accused of having trafficked women between Romania and Italy for the purpose of labour exploitation in agriculture. Victims were cheated with false promises of good, profitable legitimate employments and then forced to work in local farms, where they were underpaid and threatened. The criminal activities perpetrated by this group were: illegal intermediation with employers, subtraction of contracts, collection of payments (at higher prices) for accommodation and transportation, money extortion for residence permits and deductions from salaries (Iovino 2016). Italian OCGs, where rooted (i.e., South of Italy, and the regions of Sicily, Calabria, Apulia and Campania), make profits thanks to the control of some areas where labour exploitation takes place (IT-E16). "*In certain places, villages, gangmasters and farmers have to keep good neighbourly relations with local OCGs. This may consist in protection money and extortions*" (IT-E11) or exchanges in other criminal activities, such as drug selling. For example, in one investigative operation named "Svevia" of 2000, local OCGs active in the province of Foggia, were interested in the tomato supply, and in perpetrating money extortions to farmers of around 1000 euros for each load leaving the farm (Leogrande 2016).

Gangmasters connect demand and supply, and offer their service to farmers, thus overcoming legal ways of recruitment. "*In most cases, these persons are the only point of reference for the job searching of migrants devoid of the possibility to contact employers, and their role is crucial in less populated areas. […]. More often, they have worked for a long time in the territory and know employment mechanisms. Their activity is usually subjected to an Italian gangmaster who, in turn, is recruited by unscrupulous farmers. Differently from the past, these actors manage not only the recruitment of workers but also all aspects of their lives (i.e., hours of working, salaries)*" (Pisacane 2016: 44–45). Gangmasters operate within a criminal network. On one side they are linked to intermediaries (i.e., recruiters and travel organisers) in the countries of origin of migrants, and on the other they are in constant relation with other gangmasters and intermediaries operating in the same region or areas of Italy. One judicial investigation concerning the interceptions of two Polish gangmasters revealed connections with others collaborating for the placement of workers, and deciding the farmlands where to employ them. Some of the gangmasters charged in the trial were also involved in smuggling of solar panels, and were trying to set up operations of weapon trafficking. Another gangmaster, for example, was connected

---

rough products is almost inexistent (IT-E11; IT-E16; IT-E23). As stated by one previous victim of labour exploitation (IT-E23) "*In my opinion, the real gangmasters are food corporations that, through a mechanism of lowering costs, force farmers to resort to gangmasters to have labour force at a very low price to resist on the market*". Another reason for the use of gangmaster to hire day labourers is related to the cycles and timing of harvesting. In many cases, farmers need labour force in very short times (Ciconte and Liberti 2016).

to a friend receiving girls who wanted to work as prostitutes and paying 2500 euros for each (Leogrande 2016). Thus, as stated by an interviewed expert and as it results from investigative evidence (IT-E10) (see DIA 2017), the presence of native OCGs in the agricultural sector, known as agromafia (i.e., agricultural mafia) may favour this form of illegal employment and exploitation, and the profiting from this "criminal system", but there is not direct involvement. The lucrative business of Italian organised crime groups is to infiltrate and/or acquire legal farms, especially facing economic difficulties, in order to infiltrate or control the supply chain, such as for example imposing the purchase of specific commodities, and easily launder revenues of other criminal activities (IT-E10; IT-E11), (see Europol 2015).

Besides the very unhealthy and unsafe living and working conditions of migrants related to the higher number of working hours per day (from 12 to 14); the threats of gangmasters if they are reluctant to work; their staying in overcrowded and crumbling facilities; the neglected right to receive medical aid if needed, the majority of migrants also have their documents withheld by gangmasters. "*Seize of passports, residence permits and IDs. The declared reason is to make employment contracts, the real one is to keep us under their control. Sometimes, our documents are sold to clandestine migrants*" (Sagnet and Palmisano 2015: 29). In other cases employment contracts are absent or fictitious, or migrants are employed on piecework (IT-E15; IT-E23), (see Pisacane 2016; Iovino 2016; Leogrande 2016; MSF 2008). As contended by one expert, this option is paradoxically preferred since it allows to earn more money being paid for each filled up chest (of tomatoes, for example), (IT-E16). In general, exploiters prefer to employ foreign women since they complain less and accept lower salaries, 22 euros in front of 37 euros. A hierarchy also exists for retributions in which Caucasian workers perceive higher payments compared to African workers (Sagnet and Palmisano 2015). As stated by an interviewed victim of previous labour exploitation: "*It is hard to fight back this system. The daily threats we suffered, perpetrated by gangmasters and farmers. When the trial ended, the sentences documented the State complicity with, for example, labour inspectors informing farmers about the day of inspection*" (IT-E23).

2.4 Financing and Financial Management

As for the financial management of trafficking in human beings, the main data gathered was for Nigerian OCGs for two main reasons: nowadays in Italy they represent the most emerging criminal entrepreneurs involved in this criminal activity; the high numbers of Nigerian victims reaching the country and further exploited into prostitution, some of whom decide to collaborate with police forces and judicial institutions to escape their situation. East European OCGs have a long history in terms of sexual exploitation and are not the main and recent focus of criminal investigations. Chinese OCGs, even if investigated, are an insular ethnic group, thus allowing for more limited information to be gathered, mainly by undercover police activity.

2.4.1 *Sources of Capital for Initiating/Sustaining Operations of Trafficking in Human Beings and Profiles of Financiers*

Although Nigerian OCGs are active in the drug and sex markets, it appears that the source of financing for the trafficking operations may come from the same criminal activity or other illegal activities. As a matter of fact, the distinction is blurred when transnational OCGs are involved, and this can be true also for Eastern European criminal entrepreneurs, such as for example Albanians that operate in drug trafficking and sexual exploitation (IT-E4; IT-E10; IT-E18). Nevertheless, as underlined by one expert, Albanian OCGs when settled in Italy have started to gain profits through prostitution, and then reinvested them into drugs to be sold to Italian OCGs at a very favourable price, which allowed them to gradually ascend the hierarchical structure of this criminal market (IT-E8).

Social capital more than financial capital is crucial as to recruit potential victims in the countries of origin (IT-E4). For example, Chinese clans (i.e., extended families) are actively involved in identifying nationals that can be moved and further exploited abroad (IT-E2). In most cases, some clan members are the financiers of the trafficking operations: "*None of these Chinese migrants could leave without paying any money. It was a real extortion of OCGs against family clans that were obliged to turn to loan sharks as to pay the travel. A real form of getting into debts, but not with traffickers*" (IT-E14). Similarly, family members and relatives play a key role in recruiting Nigerian potential victims. Community relations in rural villages and other individuals in contact with the *Maman* acting as intermediaries (e.g., friends, acquaintances, priests, etc.) facilitate the process (IT-E25).

As for the financiers, there are different situations: (a) the *Maman* pays the travel and documents (if needed) in advance; (b) sponsors (i.e., persons close to the families of potential victims) that offer to cover the required expenses; (c) families or relatives that anticipate the requested money, usually getting into debts or selling their properties, and that wait to be repaid with the earnings of the victims once they have started to work in Italy (IT-E15; IT-E18; IT-E19; IT-E20; IT-E22), (see Di Nicola and Musumeci 2014). In some cases, the amount to be repaid back (i.e., the debt of the victims) is known in advance by the families and this allows to negotiate with recruiters "*in one judicial case, all the trafficked girls had to repay an amount of 30,000 euros, except for one girl for whom the family was able to agree an amount of 25,000 euros*" (IT-E4). In Libya, other required payments are needed on the side of Nigerian OCGs which have to leave the victims to other local criminal/military groups, since at present they cannot count on previous corruptive networks. Stories of women refer of the trade between Nigerian criminal entrepreneurs and Arab gangs. Victims are kept into connection or ghetto houses until the *Maman* in Italy pays this additional amount for their liberation (IT-E4; IT-E21). If she has no money when requested, victims can be bought by other *Mamans* even in Libya. "*There are ladies that go to these connection houses to buy women and girls, with the interest of profiting and making them reaching another location or country*" (IT-E4). The financiers in this occasion may also be family members or relatives, to whom more money is extorted (IT-E21). Similarly, Chinese victims are sold during their journey to Italy, even more than once, either to other members of the same OCGs, or to other criminal groups (IT-E2; IT-E14). This way, it is possible to earn more money, or to share with other criminal entrepreneurs the profits of trafficking. "*In the judicial cases handled, involving very long land routes, groups of around thirty Chinese migrants were sold several times to various criminal groups that managed different paths of the travel and that were in contact with each other*" (IT-E2). Simulated kidnapping may occur as well, and perpetrated by members of the same OCGs. This way, the anticipated amount of money is not considered, and additional money is extorted from the families or relatives of the victims (IT-E14). On the contrary, when Eastern European OCGs are involved, the recurrent scheme is the payment in advance for the travel, visas and documents (e.g., Albanians), since usually the agreement with the victims is that this amount will be repaid once starting to work in Italy (IT-E4).

2.4.2 Settlement of Payments

In general, migrants cannot leave if payments for travel and documents (when needed) are not delivered to the persons (i.e., member of OCGs, intermediaries, relatives, and acquaintances) in charge of the recruitment and arrangement of the journey, residing in the countries of origin (IT-E15). The most used way to settle payments are pre-agreed instalments, that is an initial sum of money to cover initial travel and documents expenses, and another sum of money once the victims start to work in Italy and to repay their debt. For example, in one judicial case on a Nigerian organised crime group, "*the woman (Maman) asks to [her contact] how much money is needed for the girl to arrive to Italy. The contact explains the procedure and the payment: first he will have to deposit a half of the amount to his trustee in Nigeria, and the other half when the girl will reach Italy*" (IT-E20). In another investigative operation regarding Chinese migrants, instalments were paid in three stages: "*The agreed settlement of payment was 1/3 of the total amount before the departure, another 1/3 once arrived to Italy, and a final 1/3 through working (i.e., labour exploitation)*" (IT-E14). In some cases, it also occurs that all the amount of money requested is anticipated by sponsors or family members as well as relatives before potential victims leave their country of origin (IT-E7). The agreement is then to repay once victims are employed in Italy. Sponsors, which can be also intermediaries of OCGs will be repaid by the latter or in a later moment when victims start to work (IT-E7; IT-E8). On the contrary, family members or relatives run the risk not to be repaid back. The reason is that victims are not able, in most situations, to send money to their home country because of the debt and the obligation to leave almost all the earnings to their exploiters (IT-E2; IT-E4; IT-E15; IT-E25). In the case of Nigerians, for example, the profits of victims and the possibility to send money to their families depend on their settlement in Europe and their subsequent career as *Mamans* (IT-E20).

Besides the use of cash smuggling, which is always preferred since it is less risky, when OCGs anticipate the expenses of the travel and of eventual documents for migrants, there are four main methods used to send the money to the contact person in charge of organising the journey in the country of departure (IT-E10; IT-E12; IT-E15; IT-E18; IT-E19; IT-E24):

1. *Hawala* (i.e., underground banking) which regards in particular North-Africans and Muslim populations and represents "*cash-in and cash-out businesses that primarily send personal remittances of low value, and that do not preclude sending high value business transfer*" (FATF 2013:15)[7]. Besides the separated physical transportation of money, payments are made through the use of papers with codes among trusted hawaladars (IT-E6; IT-E20).
2. *Money transfer services* (e.g., MoneyGram, Western Union, WorldRemit), especially with reference to Nigerian criminal entrepreneurs: "*in some investigations, it was evident that [the latter] hold ethnic or money transfer shops used as a cover for illicit money flows*" (IT-E12). The owners can be members of OCGs or accomplices that may borrow their ID documents or may use other customers' identity cards as to hide the number of operations per day.
3. *Postepay service*, which consists in a rechargeable credit card allowing to transfer money.
4. *Bank accounts*, where the transfer of money is delivered to bank accounts of 'strawmen', who can be family members/relatives/acquaintances or individuals connected to members of OCGs.

When trafficking involves migrants from Africa, and particularly from Nigeria, the same methods of settlement of payments are used in two other circumstances. Firstly, if more money is needed in Libya for victims to cross the Mediterranean Sea. "*The person in Nigeria appoints the smuggler for transportation and incurs a debt. It is not clear if the former sends the money from Nigeria, or if he pays through a contact in Libya. But the methods are Hawala or money transfer services*" (IT-E20). Second, when victims are kidnapped by or sold to other criminal/military groups in Libya. For example, in one judicial case, while migrants were kept prisoners in one camp in Sebha, there were persistent requests to their families to credit sums of money for their liberation through MoneyGram, Western Union or on bank accounts headed by family members (IT-E21). Unless the victims or recruiters hold a direct contact with traffickers and/or smugglers, and payments are mostly handled in cash, in all the other cases the aforementioned methods are applied. Consistently, the latter are used when paying individuals involved at the various stages and with different roles within the trafficking chain, as it occurs for example with the trolley man or boga (i.e., the person accompanying the victims from Nigeria to Libya) and the ticket man (i.e., the person in charge of recovering victims in Italy), (IT-E21; IT-E24).

[7]This type of service has been defined by the Financial Action Task Force—FATF (2013: 15) "*criminal Hawala, [a system] driven by illegitimate money flows and often controlled by criminals or criminal groups [...]. These criminal networks are characterised by high value transactions between legal and natural persons that do not necessarily share the same cultural/geographic background*".

2.4.3 Costs of Doing Business

Costs of trafficking are mainly related to travel and/or documents expenses when OCGs are the financiers both from the country of origin and through Italy to reach the final destination, and the result is not particularly high if compared to other criminal activities such as for example drug trafficking (IT-E8; IT-E15; IT-E20). In general, costs depend on the distance between the countries of origin and destination of victims, and the method (i.e., transportation) arranged for travelling (IT-E18). As reported in one judicial case on a Nigerian organised crime group, there are two ways of trafficking which are in turn related to different prices (IT-E20). The first option, which regards travelling by plane, is the safest but most expensive option since it includes the costs of the ticket, documents and corruption in the countries of origin/transit. The second, concerning the arrival to Italy by sea (crossing the desert of Niger and leaving from Libya on boats) is the cheapest, although riskier. Differences in costs of travelling encountered by traffickers reflect in diverse amounts of the debt of victims (e.g., around 50,000 euros if they arrive to Italy by plane and around 30,000 euros if they travel by land and then sea).

For victims arriving from Nigeria to Italy through the most frequent land and sea routes used by traffickers (i.e., from Benin City, crossing the desert of Niger to reach Libya and then Italy) that are subsequently exploited in the sex market, the cost of the travel ranges between 2500/3000 and 5000 euros (IT-E4; IT-E7; IT-E9; IT-E10). This amount pays the travel and the persons in charge of transportation, i.e., *passeurs* (IT-E12). It has been contended by one expert that when the amount is around 5000 euros, a part of this amount is supposed to pay the ransom requested by other groups operating in Libya that keep migrants hostages in connection or in ghetto houses (IT-E4). In some cases, additional money is required to OCGs, a sum that can range from 200 to 500 euros, as to allow victims to continue their travel to Italy (IT-E4; IT-E21). The total amount of costs for having the victims arriving to Italy can be also higher. In one case, the initial price paid by the *Maman* to her contact (i.e., partner) in Nigeria is 4000 euros, although the cost of the operation amounts to a total of 11,000: "*He explains that the money is needed for the business, and that she does not have to complain since the total amount [11,000 euros] corresponds to a favourable price. He also says that he will add to the 4,000 euros another 2,000 euros for extra expenses*" (IT-E20). A similar price for trafficking a girl from Nigeria to Italy and the city of Genoa, is reported in another judicial case, where the total amount to pay all the persons involved in her illegal entry is around 12,000 euros (IT-E20). On the contrary, other judicial evidence refers less total costs for the journey (i.e., travel, transportation, intermediate stage) which are between 500 and 800 euros (IT-E24). As for Nigerian criminal entrepreneurs, other costs are related to the voodoo rites before victims leave their country of origin: in one judicial case the price paid by the contact of the *Maman* in Nigeria is 500 euros, while from another source of information the price is 150 euros with the obligation for the victims to give another sum of money once they employed in Italy and start to repay their debt (IT-E25).

Once Nigerian victims reach Italy, there are other costs to be sustained by OCGs. Firstly, the travel to the final destination. For example, in one case the price is around 300 euros (IT-E8), although the presence of different options and routes at the national level make this estimation particularly challenging. When victims are recovered at the points of arrival (i.e., shelter centres) by a member or employee of Nigerian OCGs or the *Maman*, this person is paid around 50 euros for each travel. Second, the management of the prostitution activity such as paying the person in charge of accompanying/controlling victims on a daily basis while working (that can be Italian as well), who receive between 25 and 50 euros per day; renting of joints (i.e., open air spots located in the streets for prostitution) which cost around 50–150 euros per month and are paid to the owners that are usually other criminal entrepreneurs, e.g., Albanian OCGs (IT-E4; IT-E24). Other costs are related to the laundering of profits, and in particular to services that allow to transfer money to the countries of origin. As for Nigerians, the commission charged by the owners of money transfer services is around 1%. There are some OCGs that while using cash transportation for their profits, offer the same service to other traffickers: "*The organisation charges 6% of the transported amount that includes the delivery and concealment of money, transportation and air ticket, and final consignment. And this is also used for licit money, since preferred to money transfer services where movements can be traced*" (IT-E6). Usually, this service may occur within the Hawala system (Table 2.2).

In trafficking of human beings for labour exploitation with regard to African, Chinese and East European migrants, the costs related to the travel, the intermediation of recruitment agencies or persons in charge of providing documents and visas (both for the journey if needed, and to remain in Italy) are in general covered by the victims

Table 2.2 Indicative costs incurred by Nigerian OCG for a trafficking operation (sexual exploitation)

Type of cost	(€)
Travel from Nigeria to Italy (by land and by sea from Libya)	2500/3000–5000
Travel from Libya to Sicily (by sea)	600–1800
Voodoo rite	150–500
Ransom to criminal groups in Libya	200–500
Passeur	220–330
Travel in Italy (point of arrival to destination)	300
Ticket man	50
Accompanist/controller of girls to/at joints	25–50 euros (per day)
Renting of joints	50–150 euros (per month)
Owner of money transfer service	1–2% of the sum transferred
Money courier	6% of the sum transported

Source Authors' elaboration on gathered data, Zandonini (2017) and Commissione Parlamentare di inchiesta sul fenomeno delle mafie e sulle altre associazioni criminali, anche straniere (2017)

and no costs are sustained by criminal entrepreneurs (IT-E2; IT-E14), (see Leogrande 2016; Palmisano 2017; Sagnet and Palmisano 2015). In one case, for example, Polish migrants have paid to the recruiter or the driver of the bus a total of 200 euros, plus another sum of around 50–100 euros to other intermediaries. One Polish victim, in particular, is said to have paid 200 euros to the recruiter and other 120 euros to the driver, and then he was able to leave for Italy. In another case, a Polish man directed to the city of Foggia (region of Apulia) reports to have paid 150 euros to traffickers, 50 euros to an intermediary as to pass the last border and other 50 euros after the first week of work (see Leogrande 2016). Consistently, a Tunisian young boy had to pay 2,000 euros to an intermediary to obtain the residence permit to stay and work in Italy (Sagnet and Palmisano 2015). The actual costs are on the side of exploited victims, while profits are gained by gangmasters by reducing the final amount of salaries. In the agricultural sector, for example, the amount of wages for workers is set between the gangmasters and the farmers. While the former makes profits from detracting a part of the daily earnings of workers, and charging other costs to them (e.g., transportation, food, etc.), the latter is able to make profits due to the very low cost sustained for production. For example, drivers who bring migrants to the farmlands on a daily basis are paid 600 euros per month by gangmasters, but this cost, as explained below, is actually paid by exploited victims (Palmisano 2017; Sagnet and Palmisano 2015).

2.4.4 Profits, Spending and Money Laundering

As pointed out by Europol (2015) exact and overall estimations of profits from trafficking in human beings is challenging, and when available are unreliable. This is valid also when estimating profits of trafficking and exploitation at the national level. It is then possible to give indicative ideas of profits mainly referred to specific cases. In general, the debt incurred by the victims represents the main source of profits for OCGs. For example, the total amount of the debt for Nigerian women and girls can range between 30,000/40,000 and 50,000/60,000 euros, while for Chinese victims exploited in the sexual and labour markets is 15,000/20,000 euros (IT-E6; IT-E8; IT-E9; IT-E14; IT-E20; IT-E21) (see Di Nicola and Musumeci 2014). The requested sum of money is set arbitrarily since it does not correspond to the costs sustained for travelling, eventual documents and access to work. Nigerian OCGs may make profits by selling trafficked victims among *Mamans*, as documented by one judicial case in which one girl, once arrived in Italy, was sold to another exploiter for a price of 8000 euros (IT-E20). When the debt is repaid back, and in most cases within many years, the victims are free from their exploitative situation. When Nigerian women and girls are involved, it is more likely that they become *Mamans* and carry out the trafficking and exploitation activities using contacts previously developed. The constant arrival and employment of victims is essential for OCGs to continue making profits.

As for sexual exploitation, victims are forced to deliver daily earnings to their exploiters until the sum of the debt is repaid. Usually, they are supposed to earn a certain amount per day which can be around 100–300 euros for Nigerians and Eastern Europeans. The possibility to earn a certain amount per day is related to the ethnicity, the physical appearance and the place of working—i.e., joint (IT-E6). The sex market is highly competitive and victims, pushed to generate profits due to the debt and intimidations, can even work for very low tariffs (IT-E8; IT-E9; IT-E20). Nigerian prostitutes work for around 30 euros per service, but also for less money (around 10–15 euros). On the contrary, East European victims (Albanian and Romanian) can ask for higher tariffs, around 30-50 euros. In general, they are more good looking, they work in central areas and may have apartments where to bring clients (IT-E8; IT-E12). Reaching the daily requested amount, particularly for Nigerians, means in practice working 10–12 h a day (IT-E2; IT-E6; IT-E8; IT-E20; IT-E21). The amount of the debt for OCGs is almost a net profit due to the fact that victims have to cover the rent of houses/apartments, food and clothes expenses (IT-E8). For example, in one case (IT-E20), an exploited girl was supposed to pay 250 euros for the monthly rent plus 40 euros per week for the food. If on one side Albanian criminal entrepreneurs have adopted a more contractual approach and leave the 30–50% of the earnings to the victims, on the other Nigerians keep all of the generated income (IT-E10). As a result, exploited women and girls are able to repay their families (if they are the financiers) or to support them, once free and usually when they become *Mamans* and start to exploit other victims. For this reason, when possible, victims try to conceal a little part of their earnings and send them to their families (IT-E8). Similarly, Chinese women and girls exploited in massage centres or apartments are forced to leave all of the earnings to the owner/boss (usually a woman) until they have repaid their debt, and receive a small part of money to cover their living expenses (IT-E14). Within Nigerian OCGs, the money collector is the *Maman*, that keeps tracks of revenues and expenditures on papers or notebooks, and within the Chinese it is still a woman in charge of exploiting the girls and keeping their profits (IT-E14). In particular, the *Maman* is responsible to distribute profits to her partner or husband and to pay the other individuals that support her in managing the prostitution activity: "*the girl was used to deliver the money to this lady that, in turn, every week sent the profits to Nigeria minus the costs to pay her husband and for living expenses*" (IT-E4). It is supposed that a part of the profits is also divided with the higher level of OCGs, which involves other male members residing in Italy and other European countries (IT-E9; IT-E15).

The scheme that generates profits in labour exploitation is somehow different, and besides traffickers, there are other legal or illegal actors that make revenues within a grey economy. The first source of profiting for OCGs regards travel and document expenses that are covered by migrants. The latter usually pay the recruitment agencies in the country of origin and, in some cases, in Italy. Available examples are related to different economic sectors: 200 euros each month are remitted by a caregiver employed in Italy; 700 euros a year are paid by a waitress working in a Hotel on the Italian coast, 200 euros to a Polish recruiter to work in agriculture (Palmisano 2017).

In the agricultural sector, while farmers profit from employing labour force at low cost (and this is valid also for processing companies and corporations within an 'adulterated' production system), illegal profits from labour exploitation are mainly made by gangmasters, employers (when recruitment agencies are involved), and the owners of the lands where accommodations for workers are located (IT-E10; IT-E15), (see Sagnet and Palmisano 2015; Palmisano 2017; Ciconte and Liberti 2016). As for farmers, earnings are still high and allow to remain on the market as previously explained. The following example is indicative: "*They told us that we would have been paid 3 euros for each chest of tomatoes.*[8] *Five workers were able to gather 25 chests per day, each of them earning 15 euros and each chest containing 2,8 tons of tomatoes. 25 chests a day are equal to a total of 70 tons of tomatoes. Since farmer will sell each ton for 60 euros, profit margins are high*" (Leogrande 2016: 98).

Illegal profits of gangmasters are significant. In the area of Capitanata (located in the province of Foggia of the region of Apulia, Leogrande (2016: 204) reports the following example: "*if the gangmaster subtracts 50 cents per hour from the salary of day labourers (paid in some cases also 2,80 euros instead of 3,00 euros) after 10 h of work, he has gained 5 euros. If workers are 50, the amount increases to 250 euros. In a month he profits 7,500 euros*". A Chinese criminal entrepreneur was used to subtract sums of money from salaries of the victims in order to provide them with employment contracts and residence permits, and to have their debt repaid. "*This boss usually told the victims, you have to pay me a total of 15,000 euros for your travel and documents, and to remain in Italy. Thus, you own me 1,000 for the residence; 1,000 euros for the person that works in the Prefecture; 1,000 for the policeman that helps me; 100 euros are needed to pay the representatives of the cooperative that found you an employment*" (IT-E14). The monthly amount of salaries was settled between this boss and the representatives of the employment cooperative: "*if the boss needed, for example, to legalise three Chinese migrants he agreed fictitious contracts of an amount of 1,000 per month. Out of this sum, 500 euros were for the worker and the other 500 euros were kept to pay governmental contributions as well as the debt and other costs for documents to remain in Italy*" (IT-E14).

As for the agricultural sector, daily salaries are decided between farmers and gangmasters, the former pay around 4–5 euros for one chest, the latter detract 1.50 euros. An interviewed victim (previously exploited), refers that they should have been paid 5.00 euros for each chest of tomatoes gathered but that the actual amount was 3.00 euros, with 1.50 euros subtracted by the gangmaster. A worker was able to fill 6–7 chests a day (IT-E23). Although gangmasters sustain costs related to minivans, drivers, rent of accommodations and salaries of their assistants, the main part of expenses are recovered from employees. As an example, Leogrande (2016) reports an indicative estimation of profits equal to 1 million and a half euros in two years (2005–2006) considering a total of 5000 Polish workers in the farmlands of the region of Apulia and a mean of one month of employment for each worker, from whom 5 euros a day are subtracted by gangmasters.

[8] As suggested elsewhere (Leogrande 2016; Sagnet and Palmisano 2015), these wages (i.e., 3 euros per chest, or 3.50 euros per hour) are not aligned with national contract agreements for this type of work (4.40 euros as a minimum threshold for 6 and a half working hours per day).

Charges of gangmasters are related to clothes used for working; accommodations (30–50 euros per month to the owner of the land), food (4 euros per day); mobile recharging (50 cents); shower (1 euro); medical aid (5 euros to be brought to the hospital). Penalties maybe also applied, such as 20 euros a day if workers do not respect the arbitrary time of picking tomatoes. "*From my daily salary of 20–25 euros, he subtracted 5 euros for transportation to the farmland; 3,5 euros for a sandwich and 1.50 euros for water. We actually received a net salary of 10 euros per each working day of 12-14 h*" (IT-E23). With regards to an Algerian gangmaster, it is reported that he was used to bring employees to bars, restaurants and supermarkets he owned, or to others of Italian accomplices where food and different products were charged three times more than the market price (Palmisano 2017).

It has also to be noted that it is not so uncommon that salaries are not paid to victims, and this means that their daily/monthly earnings are entirely kept by gangmasters which in turn increase their profits. The latter may be involved in other criminal activities while exploiting foreign and Italian workers, such as drug supply within farmlands. For example, the consumption of amphetamine by Polish migrants, and especially to sustain the very heavy working conditions has been reported. Gangmasters acquire the drug at the wholesale level for a price of 7 euros per gram and resell it at 30 euros per gram, which is a price higher than the mean daily salary of workers. The latter may work for free to repay the drug. "*In one occasion, my gangmaster bought around 160 grams and due to the difference in prices, he profited 3,000 euros in few days*" (Leogrande 2016: 189).

At present, the investigative and judicial evidence suggests that, after living expenses and the costs for running the business, revenues are reinvested to run the same criminal activity, and in drug trafficking especially with reference to Albanians and Nigerians OCGs. In general, net profits are sent to the countries of origin for two main reasons: either to finance new trafficking operations or to invest in real estates and commercial activities (hotels, restaurants, bars, etc.), and this is valid, with very few exceptions, for all the foreign OCGs (IT-E1; IT-E2; IT-E4; IT-E6; IT-E12; IT-E14; IT-E20). For example, Polish gangmasters, involved in labour exploitation used profits to acquire real estates both in Poland and Italy: one of those "*well settled in Italy and willing to stay, besides showing his wealth as every parvenu, has started to invest big shares in pubs, bars, apartments, cars, shops. In one year he bought a house [and] paid 160,000 euros in cash*" (Leogrande 2016: 206). Compared to other foreign criminal entrepreneurs, Chinese OCGs invest revenues in Italy, and this allows to root in local territories, launder profits, and keep running their legal and illegal economies. In one case, a Chinese boss opened bank accounts, and acquired houses and apartments thanks also to the conspiracy of bank directors and notaries. "*Using copies of the documents of exploited migrants he opened bank accounts, made notary deeds, and to put the signature it was not the documented Chinese but another national paid 200 euros for this service*". One migrant, "*after having repaid his debt and requesting a mortgage to a bank as to buy an apartment, discovered to be the holder of three houses and of negative bank accounts*" (IT-E14). Notwithstanding this, a part of profits is sent back to their country of origin: "*The system used was the concealment of cash transported by plane. There was a list of individuals with this role and working for Chinese criminal entrepreneurs. The typical route is leaving from Italy to Portugal or Spain and from there to China. Once, a man arrived to Lisbon to recover a suitcase with 600,000 euros, then he was leaving by plane to Beijing to deliver the money and returned to Rome. He was used to travel 3-4 times a year. These are trusted men, well known to transfer money, which is the most important criminal activity, and also related to the Hawala system*" (IT-E14).

The same method and other money transfer systems, are employed by Nigerian OCGs that, contrary to Chinese ones, invest all the revenues in their country of origin (IT-E1; IT-E2; IT-E6; IT-E19) to acquire properties and commercial activities for themselves or family members: "*my Maman used the money I gave her, 11,000 euros to finish her house in Nigeria*" (IT-E21). More in general, revenues of trafficking in human beings sustain the economy of some African states. It is documented, for example, that almost the entire economy of Benin City is supported by the money made through this illicit activity, when the first migrants arrived to Europe and understood its potential for money making (IT-E25), (see Musumeci and Rosini 2017; Carchedi 2016).

Nigerians prefer to "*transport cash, through individuals called also trolley men, which arrive last minute to the airport with 8–9 of big suitcases wrapped in cellophane. Confident in the very limited time, they risk less control from customs officers and manage to transport this well concealed money*" (IT-E6). The small part of profits invested in Italy is for buying or renting ethnic shops or bazaars that in many cases are covert places offering services such as money transfers used by *Mamans* or her assistants (IT-E4). Another scheme used to send profits to the country of origin is called "Euro to Euro", an informal system to transfer values based on services and guarantees *ad personam* (i.e., linked to the credibility of the intermediary) within a widespread network of individuals located mainly in Nigeria, and with money collectors in Italy (IT-E4; IT-21). Its functioning is explained as follows: "*A first man calls the [Maman] that refers to him the account details [i.e., codes] of the Euro to Euro payment. Then, the same man calls another person to communicate the received account details. The latter will communicate this information in Nigeria as soon as he has finished to work. The first man calls back the [Maman] and confirms to have reported the received information, and that the person expecting the money in Nigeria will go on Monday*" (IT-E21). Similarly, Eastern European OCGs, invest profits in their home countries to acquire real estates, commercial properties (e.g., bar, restaurants, pubs, hotels) and companies, using mainly cash transportation and money transfer services. A smaller part of revenues or the total amount (in case of small criminal groups) is spent for a lavish lifestyle. "*In one investigation on Albanian and Romanian criminal entrepreneurs, it was evident the fast change of luxury cars, and profits were mainly used to show off a high standard of life. They do not hold a particular dynamic entrepreneurial spirit if compared to drug traffickers*" (IT-E1).

2.5 Conclusion

Due to its geographical position, Italy represents a key area for migration flows especially from North and West Africa through Central Mediterranean Sea, followed by Eastern European countries and China. Among these arrivals, the available estimations although not comprehensive, suggest that a part of migrants are further exploited for sexual or labour purposes, due to the presence of more or less organised OCGs involved in trafficking in human beings. Sexual exploitation is managed by the Nigerian, Chinese, Albanian and Romanian criminal entrepreneurs; while labour exploitation mainly by the Eastern Europeans and Chinese, with Italian nationals benefitting from this exploitation. These actors share similar organisational characteristics: they are small in size (from 3–4 to 10–15 members) and operate within large, fluid and horizontal criminal networks based on nodes present in the countries of origin of victims and destination. Members are linked by family, ethnic and tribal bonds. Hubs for sexual exploitation are located in different Italian cities such as Turin, Milan (North); Naples, Castel Volturno and Palermo (South). Labour exploitation occurs mainly in the agricultural sector and in the province of Foggia—i.e., the area of Capitanata located in the region of Apulia. Collaborations among foreign OCGs exist, such as between Albanians and Romanians in the sex market, and the exchange of favours or services are requested if these actors operate in areas under the control of Italian OCGs. The latter are involved in other criminal activities (e.g. drug trafficking, tobacco smuggling) considered to be more profitable and less risky.

Thus, foreign OCGs have not encountered particular barriers to enter these criminal markets in Italy, as it occurs in managing trafficking operations. Recruitment is facilitated by social capital in terms of networks of family members, friends or acquaintances, or by fake advertisements of job opportunities on the web and social media. The expenses for travel and documents (when needed) in most cases are sustained by the victims or their families, especially if labour exploitation is concerned. Even if OCGs advance this sum of money, including through sponsors that are in contact with them, the costs are much less than the profits gained. In the case of sexual exploitation, the amount of the debts of the victims imposed for their liberation is set completely arbitrarily and largely encompasses the costs incurred. Similarly, with regard to labour exploitation, the earnings of the gangmasters that illegally keep part of workers' daily salaries are significant. Profits are mainly used to run other trafficking operations, although in some cases can finance other criminal activities, as it happens with drug trafficking by the Nigerian and Albanian criminal entrepreneurs. The revenues of trafficking in human beings are mainly reinvested in the countries of origin to acquire real estates, bars, restaurants, companies, and a small part is spent in Italy for living expenses or to sustain a lavish lifestyle. The methods employed to transfer the profits are similar to those used for the settlement of payments—paying the individuals involved in the trafficking operations and in the exploitation activities. In particular, cash transportation represents the most frequent way of payment, together with the use of money transfer services and informal banking systems such as the hawala.

References

Amnesty International. (2015). *'Libya is full of cruelty'. Stories of abduction, sexual violence and abuse from migrants and refugees*. Available at http://www.amnesty.eu/content/assets/Reports_and_Briefings_2015/Libya_is_full_of_cruelty.pdf.

Baldoni, E. (2011). Scenari emergenti nella tratta a scopo di sfruttamento sessuale verso l'Italia. *Revista Interdisciplinar da Mobilidade Humana – REMHU, 19*(37), 43–58.

Becucci, S. (2016). La criminalità organizzata cinese. Costanti, cambiamenti, e aspetti controversi. In S. Becucci & F. Carchedi (Eds.), *Mafie straniere in Italia. Come operano, come si contrastano* (pp. 59–89). Milano: FrancoAngeli.

Beretta, L., Bondì, L., De Masi, F., Esposito, F., Festagallo, F., Gargano, O., et al. (Eds.). (2016). *Inter/rotte. Storie di tratta, percorsi di resistenze*. Roma: BeFree Cooperativa Sociale contro Tratta, Violenze, Discriminazioni, Edizioni Sapere Solidale.

Bertolotti, C. (2017, December 26). Come funziona il racket dell'elemosina della mafia nigeriana. *Panorama*. Available at https://www.panorama.it/news/cronaca/come-funziona-il-racket-dellelemosina-della-mafia-nigeriana/.

Cabras, F. (2015). Il racket della prostituzione a Torino e Genova. Strutture, strategie e trasformazioni. *Polis, 3,* 365–390.

Campana, P., & Varese, F. (2015). Exploitation in human trafficking and smuggling. *European Journal on Criminal Policy and Research, 22*(1), 89–105.

Carchedi, F. (2010). *La tratta delle minorenni nigeriane in Italia. I dati, i racconti, i servizi sociali.* UNICRI. Available at http://www.piemonteimmigrazione.it/site/images/stories/tratta/documenti/TrattaMinorenniNigeriaItalia_IT.pdf.

Carchedi, F. (2016). La criminalità transnazionale nigeriana. Alcuni aspetti strutturali. In S. Becucci & F. Carchedi (Eds.), *Mafie straniere in Italia. Come operano, come si contrastano* (pp. 29–55). Milano: FrancoAngeli.

Carchedi, F., & Tola, V. (2005). *Sintesi del rapporto finale del progetto per una ricerca-azione su prostituzione straniera e traffico di donne a scopo di sfruttamento sessuale. Analisi delle trasformazioni correnti nei principali gruppi nazionali coinvolti e nuove strategie di intervento di protezione sociale. Il caso dell'area metropolitana di Roma*. Parsec-Consortium. Available at https://www.comune.roma.it/PCR/resources/cms/documents/Parsec_1.pdf.

Ciconte, E. (2016). La criminalità mafiosa albanese. Un fenomeno da approfondire. In S. Becucci & F. Carchedi (Eds.), *Mafie straniere in Italia. Come operano, come si contrastano* (pp. 96–107). Milano: FrancoAngeli.

Ciconte, F., & Liberti, S. (2016). *Spolpati. La crisi dell'industria del pomodoro tra sfruttamento e insostenibilità. Terzo rapporto della campagna – Filiera sporca*. Available at http://www.filierasporca.org/wp-content/uploads/2016/11/Terzo-Rapporto-Filierasporca_WEB1.pdf.

Commissione Parlamentare di inchiesta sul fenomeno delle mafie e sulle altre associazioni criminali, anche straniere. (2017). *Relazione su mafie, migranti e tratta di esseri umani, nuove forme di schiavitù*. Available at https://www.senato.it/service/PDF/PDFServer/DF/336112.pdf.

Curtol, F., Decarli, S., Di Nicola, A., & Savona, E. U. (2004). Victims of human trafficking in Italy: A judicial perspective. *International Review of Victimology, 11*(1), 111–141.

Di Nicola, A., & Musumeci, G. (2014). *Confessioni di un trafficante di uomini*. Milano: Chiarelettere.

Di Nicola, A., Baratto, G., Martini, E. (2017). *Surf and Sound. The role of the internet in people smuggling and human trafficking*. eCrime Research Reports 03, University of Trento. Available at http://www.surfandsound.eu/.

DIA—Direzione Investigativa Antimafia. (2017). *Attività svolta e risultati conseguiti dalla Direzione Investigativa Antimafia. Gennaio – Giugno 2017*. Available at http://direzioneinvestigativaantimafia.interno.gov.it/semestrali/sem/2017/1sem2017.pdf.

Department of Equal Opportunities. (2018). *Dati – Contro la tratta*. Available at https://www.youtube.com/watch?v=8eB8uiDCLS8&feature=youtu.be.

DNA—Direzione Nazionale Antimafia e Antiterrorismo. (2017). *Relazione annuale sulle attività svolte dal Procuratore nazionale e dalla Direzione nazionale antimafia e antiterrorismo nonché sulle dinamiche e strategie della criminalità organizzata di tipo mafioso nel periodo 1 luglio – 30 giugno 2016*. Available at http://www.avvisopubblico.it/home/wp-content/uploads/2017/06/RELAZIONE-DNA-1.7.2015-30.6.2016.pdf.

Eastwest.eu. (2013, June 27). *Come si muove la mafia cinese sul territorio italiano*. Available at http://eastwest.eu/attachments/article/851/east22_Come_si_muove_la_mafia_cinese_sul_territorio_italiano.pdf.

European Commission. (2018a). *Italy 2. Institutional and legal framework*. Available at https://ec.europa.eu/anti-trafficking/member-states/italy-2-institutional-and-legal-framework_en.

European Commission. (2018b). *Italy 3. Implementation of anti-trafficking policy*. Available at https://ec.europa.eu/anti-trafficking/member-states/italy-3-implementation-anti-trafficking-policy_en.

Europol. (2015). *Trafficking in human beings in the EU. Situation Report*. Available at https://www.europol.europa.eu/publications-documents/trafficking-in-human-beings-in-eu.

Eurostat. (2015). *Trafficking in human beings*. Available at https://ec.europa.eu/anti-trafficking/sites/antitrafficking/files/eurostat_report_on_trafficking_in_human_beings_-_2015_edition.pdf.

FATF—Financial Action Task Force. (2013). *FATF Report. The role of Hawala and other similar service providers in money laundering and terrorist financing*. Available at http://www.fatf-gafi.org/media/fatf/documents/reports/Role-of-hawala-and-similar-in-ml-tf.pdf.

FRONTEX—European Border and Coast Guard Agency. (2017). *Risk analysis for 2017*. Available at https://frontex.europa.eu/assets/Publications/Risk_Analysis/Annual_Risk_Analysis_2017.pdf.

FRONTEX—European Border and Coast Guard Agency. (2018). *Risk analysis for 2018*. Available at https://frontex.europa.eu/publications/risk-analysis-for-2018-aJ5nJu.

Goisis, L. (2016). *L'immigrazione clandestina e il delitto di tratta di esseri umani. Smuggling of migrants e trafficking in persons: la disciplina italiana*. Diritto Penale Contemporaneo. Available at https://www.penalecontemporaneo.it/upload/GOISIS_2016a.pdf.

GRETA—Group of Experts on Action against Trafficking in Human Beings. (2016). *Report on Italy under Rule 7 of the Rules of Procedure for evaluating the implementation of the Council of Europe Convention on Action against Trafficking in Human Beings*. Available at http://rm.coe.int/16806edf35.

GRETA—Group of Experts on Action against Trafficking in Human Beings. (2019). *Report concerning the implementation of the Council of Europe Convention on Action against Trafficking in Human Beings by Italy. Second evaluation round*. Available at https://www.osservatoriointerventitratta.it/wp-content/uploads/2019/01/GRETA_2018_28_FGR_ITA.pdf.pdf.

Ingrascì, O. (2016). La criminalità mafiosa russa, ucraina e georgiana. In S. Becucci & F. Carchedi (Eds.), *Mafie straniere in Italia. Come operano, come si contrastano* (pp. 109–123). Milano: FrancoAngeli.

IOM—International Organization for Migration. (2017). *La tratta di esseri umani attraverso la rotta del mediterraneo centrale: dati, storie e informazioni raccolte dall'organizzazione internazionale per le migrazioni*, available at http://www.italy.iom.int/sites/default/files/news-documents/RAPPORTO_OIM_Vittime_di_tratta_0.pdf.

IOM—International Organization for Migration. (2018a). *Mediterranean migrant arrivals reached 171,635 in 2017; Deaths reach 3116*. Available at https://www.iom.int/news/mediterranean-migrant-arrivals-reached-171635-2017-deaths-reach-3116.

IOM—International Organization for Migration. (2018b). *Flow monitoring Europe*. Available at http://migration.iom.int/europe?type=arrivals.

IOM—International Organization for Migration. (2018c). *Mixed migration flows in the Mediterranean, Compilation of Available Data and Information. November 2018*. Available at file:///Users/fiamma/Downloads/Flows_Compilation_Report_November_2018_0.pdf.

Iovino, R. (2016). Le agromafie e il caporalato: liberiamoci dall'illegalità, restituiamo dignità al lavoro. In *Agromafie e Caporalato. Terzo Rapporto* (pp. 15–31). Roma: Osservatorio Placido Rizzotto, Ediesse.

Leogrande, A. (2016). *Uomini e caporali. Viaggio tra I nuovi schiavi nelle campagne del Sud.* Milano: Giangiacomo Feltrinelli Editore.

Mancuso, M. (2013). Not all madams have a central role: Analysis of a Nigerian sex trafficking network. *Trends in Organized Crime, 17*(1–2), 66–88.

MEDU—Doctors for Human Rights. (2018). *EXODI. Migratory routes from Sub-Saharan Countries to Europe*. Available at http://esodi.mediciperidirittiumani.org/en/#all.

MSF—Medici Senza Frontiere Italia. (2008). *Una stagione all'inferno. Rapporto sulle condizioni degli immigrati impiegati in agricoltura nelle regioni del Sud Italia.* Available at http://archivio.medicisenzafrontiere.it/allegati/pubblicazioni/rapporti/una_stagione_all_inferno.pdf.

MSNBC. (2018). *Libya as a gateway*. Available at http://www.msnbc.com/specials/migrant-crisis/libya.

Ministero dell'Interno. (2015). *Relazione sull'attività delle forze di polizia, sullo stato dell'ordine e della sicurezza pubblica e sulla criminalità organizzata.* Senato della Repubblica, XVII Legislatura. Available at http://www.parlamento.it/service/PDF/PDFServer/BGT/1007661.pdf.

Musumeci, G., & Rosini, G. (2017, November 24). La tratta delle Nigeriane. Benin City l'orrore che ignoriamo. *Sette. Corriere della Sera.* Available at http://www.corriere.it/sette/17_novembre_23/benin-city-nigeria-tratta-prostituzione-l-orrore-che-ignoriamo-da1e1f60-ce02-11e7-a3ca-40392580f143.shtml.

Palmisano, L. (2017). *Mafia Caporale*. Roma: Fandango Libri.

Pisacane, L. (2016). Immigrazione e mercato del lavoro agricolo. In Osservatorio Placido Rizzotto (Ed.), *Agromafie e Caporalato. Terzo Rapporto* (pp. 33–43). Roma: Osservatorio Placido Rizzotto.

Politi, J., & Fick, M. (2015, December 3). The long and dangerous road to slavery. Traffickers are luring Nigerian women to Italy and entrapping more and more in the sex trade. *Financial Times*. Available at https://www.ft.com/content/26f1a120-990f-11e5-95c7-d47aa298f769.

Reitano, T., Adal, L., & Shaw, M. (2014). *Smuggled futures. The dangerous path of the migrant from Africa to Europe*. The Global Initiative against Transnational Organized Crime. Available at http://www.integrazionemigranti.gov.it/Attualita/Notizie/Documents/Global%20Initiative.pdf.

Russo, G. (2010). La mafia Albanese. *Rassegna Italiana di Criminologia, 1,* 1–10.

Sagnet, Y., & Palmisano, L. (2015). *Ghetto Italia. I braccianti stranieri tra caporalato e sfruttamento*. Roma: Fandango Libri.

Save the Children. (2017). *Piccoli schiavi invisibili. I minori stranieri vittime di tratta e sfruttamento in Italia.* Available at https://www.savethechildren.it/sites/default/files/files/uploads/pubblicazioni/piccoli-schiavi-invisibili-2017.pdf.

Scotto, A. (2016). Between exploitation and protest: Migrants and the agricultural gangmaster system in Southern Italy. *Revista Interdisciplinar da Mobilidade Humana—REMHU, 48*, 79–92. Available at http://www.scielo.br/pdf/remhu/v24n48/1980-8585-REMHU-24-48-079.pdf.

Shelley, L. (2014). *Human smuggling and trafficking into Europe. A comparative perspective*. Migration Policy Institute. Available at http://www.migrationpolicy.org/research/human-smuggling-and-trafficking-europe-comparative-perspective.

Spiezia, F. (2008). *La tratta di esseri umani: gli strumenti investigativi di cooperazione internazionale*. Available at http://briguglio.asgi.it/immigrazione-e-asilo/2009/agosto/art-spiezia-traff-ess-um.pdf.

UNODC—United Nations Office on Drugs and Crime. (2013). *Transnational organized crime in East Asia and the Pacific. A threat assessment*. Available at http://www.unodc.org/res/cld/bibliography/transnational-organized-crime-in-east-asia-and-the-pacific-a-threat-assessment_html/TOCTA_EAP_web.pdf.

Wittenberg, L. (2017). *Managing mixed migration: The central mediterranean route to Europe*. International Peace Institute, New York. Available at https://www.ipinst.org/wp-content/uploads/2017/04/1704_Managing-Mixed-Migration.pdf.

Zandonini, G. (2017). *Non sono un criminale: storia di un ex passeur del Niger*. Open Migration. Available at https://openmigration.org/analisi/non-sono-un-criminale-storia-di-un-ex-passeur-del-niger/.

Chapter 3
Human Trafficking and Its Financial Management in the United Kingdom

3.1 Introduction

The UK is primarily a destination country for trafficking victims from central and southeastern Europe, the Commonwealth of Independent States (CIS), Africa, Asia, Latin America, and the Caribbean. There have also been cases in which the UK was a *transit* and *source* country for trafficking victims (see Cockbain 2018; Brayley and Cockbain 2014). In a rather unusual case, in 2008, the UK Human Trafficking Centre (UKHTC) identified vulnerable British nationals, who were trafficked by a British crime 'collectivity' to Norway. They were subjected to labour exploitation and were paid as little as £20 per week (Home Office 2009). Although in UK policy, law enforcement and non-governmental organisation (NGO) rationale great emphasis is placed on human trafficking that is of transnational nature, it is important for one to remember that human trafficking is not always and necessarily a transnational crime. Indeed, in local, multi-agency settings in the country, domestic/internal trafficking has been also recognised as an issue affecting UK and British nationals and at an increasing rate (UK-E4; UK-E5; UK-E6; UK-E7; UK-E13; UK-E14, etc.).

The purpose of this chapter is to provide an account of the financial management of the human trafficking business in the UK, an area that is largely under-researched (see Zhang 2009). Following this introduction, the chapter is based on four substantive sections:

- Section 3.2 provides a general overview of the human trafficking business and discusses existing relations between the legitimate sectors and human trafficking in the UK;
- Section 3.3 offers an account of the social organisation of human trafficking in the UK and the key actors involved;
- Section 3.4 describes the financial aspects of human trafficking in terms of source of financing, settlement of payments, costs of business, as well as the profits made and how the profits are spent and further invested. Finally, it examines the role of the internet in the human trafficking business and its finances.

G. A. Antonopoulos et al., *Human Trafficking Finances*, SpringerBriefs in Criminology, https://doi.org/10.1007/978-3-030-17809-3_3

- Finally, Sect. 3.5 examines the role of the internet in the human trafficking business and its finances.

3.2 Market Overview

The British Government, through a "multiple systems estimation" approach, which analyses the overlaps between human trafficking cases that come to the attention of the authorities through various sources, estimates that there are between 10,000 and 13,000 *potential* victims of human trafficking (in all its forms) in the country (see Silverman 2014). Of course, it is extremely difficult to determine accurately the scale of trafficking in the UK (and any other context), and have a clear picture as to the numbers of people who have been trafficked, due to the clandestine nature of human trafficking, underreporting, (often) culturally-induced reluctance to report victimisation to the authorities, "…significant intelligence gaps on human trafficking…" (UK-E9), lack of awareness and understanding of the signs of human trafficking (Hornsby et al. 2017), as well as discrepancies in statistical reports (see also Kelly and Regan 2000; Goodey 2008; Project Acumen 2010; Weitzer 2012). The official estimate admittedly is based on "very poor data around the number of people trafficked, and hence [there are] large margins for errors"…; "the analysis is based on estimates concerning the proportion of women involved in prostitution who are likely to have been trafficked ([and] it [is] not directly informed by evidence concerning the number of women observed to have been trafficked)" (Dubourg and Prichard 2008: iii and 15). After 2009, the number of *potential* victims of human trafficking is a product of the National Referral Mechanism (NRM).[1] Between its inception in 2009 and December 2016 14,538 people were referred to the National Referral Mechanism (Table 3.1).

Table 3.1 Number of potential victims referred to the National Referral Mechanism, 2009–2016

Year	2009[a]	2010	2011	2012	2013	2014	2015	2016
Referrals	535	714	946	1186	1746	2340	3266	3805

[a]2009 figures cover April–December only
Sources Home Office (2014), NCA (2015, 2017a)

[1]"The National Referral Mechanism is a framework for identifying victims of human trafficking or modern slavery and ensuring they receive the appropriate support. The NRM is also the mechanism through which the Modern Slavery Human Trafficking Unit (MSHTU) collects data about victims. This information contributes to building a clearer picture about the scope of human trafficking and modern slavery in the UK. The NRM was introduced in 2009 to meet the UK's obligations under the Council of Europe Convention on Action against Trafficking in Human Beings. At the core of the NRM is the process of locating and identifying "potential victims of trafficking" " (NCA 2017b). To be referred into the NRM, potential victims must be referred by an authorised agency, known as the "first responder" (police, border force, GLA, local authorities, specific NGOs) to a "competent authority" (the UKHTC or Home Office Immigration and Visas—where trafficking may be an issue as part of an asylum claim).

In 2016, there were 3805 potential victims submitted to the NRM, a 17% increase on 2015 figures, which were in turn a 40% increase on 2014 figures. Of these 3805 potential victims, 1936 were female (51%), 1864 (48%) were male and a further 5 (<1%) were recorded as "transgender." Reporting showed potential victims of trafficking from 108 countries, with Albanian, UK and Vietnamese nationals being the most commonly reported nationalities (NCA 2017a). In 487 cases the type of exploitation was recorded as "unknown." The number of underage victims was 1278, the majority of whom were from the UK (255 children), an increase of 100.8% from 2015 (NCA 2017a). One needs to be reminded that these are people referred into the NRM and are not necessarily confirmed as trafficking victims.[2] In fact, the Independent Anti-Slavery Commissioner in his first annual report noted that just over a quarter of the cases identified in England and Wales in 2015 under the NRM resulted in crimes recorded by the police (The Guardian 2016). Moreover, according to a recent report by the National Audit Office, 46% of all referrals made in 2016 had not received a *conclusive* grounds decision as at March 2017 (National Audit Office 2017).

According to Organised Crime Group (OCG) Mapping, in 2015 there were over 6000 active OCGs consisting of nearly 50,000 individuals (NCA 2016). However, there is no estimate of the OCGs that are involved in human trafficking in particular, and even if this was the case, the estimate would inevitably ignore the large number of *individual* traffickers. Network analyses of the trafficking cases known to the Greater Manchester Police in 2015, for instance, suggested that most suspects were individuals involved in just one crime of exploitation against one victim (Gadd et al. 2017; see also following section).

The number of prosecutions for "human trafficking"/"modern slavery" offences[3] is increasing (especially following from the Modern Slavery Act 2015) against a relatively low base compared to the referrals (see also Haughey 2016). In 2015, for example, 117 offenders were prosecuted for modern slavery offences in the UK, 19% higher than the 98 prosecuted in 2014. From 2004 to 2015, 511 individuals were convicted for human trafficking/modern slavery offences (see Table 3.2).

At least three phases can be distinguished in the human trafficking process: (a) recruitment; (b) transportation from the place of origin to the place of destination and potentially the illegal entry of the trafficked person; and (c) the exploitation phase (see Salt and Stein 1997). The first phase, *recruitment*, excluding the event of

Table 3.2 Number of convictions for human trafficking/modern slavery offences in the UK, 2004–2015

Year	2004	2005	2006	2007	2008	2009	2010	2011	2012	2013	2014	2015
Convictions	0	12	21	23	24	25	16	8	13	148	108	113

Sources Haughey (2016: 13); www.parliament.uk

[2]In addition, there is no link between these referrals, and arrests and convictions.

[3]"Modern slavery" was introduced as a separate crime recording category in April 2015.

abduction of the victim, is known to be facilitated by a diverse set of actors as friends and family of the victim, co-workers, people of spiritual authority, employment agencies, or even artistic management companies (UK-E1; UK-E2; UK-E3; UK-E4; UK-E5; UK-E5, UK-V1 etc.). In some cases, the context of the recruitment phase is informal networks in small localities in the country of origin. For instance, a significant number of trafficking victims from Romania in a locality in the north of England are recruited in Pentecostal churches in specific villages or small towns in the country in which there is an over-representation of Roma people; villages such as Calaras, Bacau, Vrancea, Focsani etc. (UK-E11). In many cases in the recruitment phase, traffickers take advantage of local financial and cultural peculiarities in the country of origin:

> So there, the understanding is, Vietnam, poor family, organised criminals in Vietnam say 'right, we'll give you whatever [payment], this is your money, send so and so [the trafficked victim(s)] to the UK, they're now going to pay off the debt'. What that means for us is that we've now got a safeguarding issue because they're a child, a child who won't comply, because generally, a child from Vietnam, they're much more streetwise than our kids, you've got a child who feels it is an honour to pay back the family debt, you've got a child who feels that their family will be seriously harmed or murdered if they don't pay off the debt, and you have a child who probably still think that their life is still better here than it was in Vietnam. (UK-E5)

Traffickers may use legitimate agencies but even when an illegitimate front is used, they may present to the victim contracts and legal documentation as a means of alleviating any concerns about trafficking and masking the intended exploitation (UK-E1; UK-E2; UK-E3). Many of the exploited individuals are knowingly and voluntarily recruited for both the sex industry and the labour market in the UK. Although they know or suspect the labour sector they would be introduced in, they may be unaware of the level of exploitation. Forging documents or obtaining the necessary documents, by means of corruption and bribery of law enforcement or other officials is a possibility at this stage. The recruitment phase also involves false promises including "employment packages" where they are also offered (tied) accommodation as part of their job, as well as various provisions and help with everyday life practicalities. For example, most Romanian people who come in the north of England for work are promised—apart from work on a contractual basis—help with the process of claiming benefits and health care (such as the services of a dentist). In the case of internal trafficking in the UK, recruitment very often involves homeless people, poor people hanging out in food banks and "soup kitchens," individuals with mental health problems (Oram et al. 2015) and dependencies, and grooming (vulnerable) children and young people at care facilities (UK-E7). Interestingly, one of the research participants mentioned that an individual, who had been identified by the local police as a trafficking "risk," attempted at joining Barnardo's SECOS (Sexual Exploitation Children's Outreach Service) Project on a voluntary basis in order to have access to potential victims (UK-E4). Finally, recruitment is also facilitated by information and communication technologies (see also Sect. 3.5).

Transportation, including the stage of harbouring the victims in transit, is also a phase in which different actors perform different functions (see following section)—the financial significance being that the involvement of a variety of actors entails transactions, which cannot be indiscriminately considered as part of an "organised crime activity". The transportation to the UK, especially from other EU member states, is frequently executed legally. In the case of non-EU nationals, transportation involves mostly ports in the south and east coasts of the country (UK-E5).

There are two main forms of *exploitation*—(a) *sexual exploitation* and (b) *labour exploitation*—being relatively more visible and thus detectable than other forms of human trafficking, such as, for instance, organ harvesting and trafficking. Sex trafficking victims can be highly visible and engage in street-level prostitution but in many cases sex trafficking takes place in "underground" venues, such as private homes or brothels. Public and *legitimate* locations such as massage parlours, spas, health clubs, and strip clubs also act as fronts for illegal prostitution and trafficking.[4] Similarly, forced labour has been detected in labour intensive manufacture, construction and agriculture (e.g. fruit farms in Kent, cockle farms in Cumbria etc.) (see also UNODC 2009), service establishments such as nails salons, car washes, garages, cleaning services, tanning salons, the hospitality industry, restaurants, the care industry, skip hire companies and waste disposals as well as domestic servitude.[5] What facilitates labour trafficking and exploitation in the UK is the extended labour supply chains, which allow for a high degree of separation between the agent (intermediary) who supplies labour, on one hand, and the end-user of labour, on the other. In such a diverse and devolved system, legal businesses are not always aware of where the workers were sourced and how they were recruited (Harris et al. 2014; Skrivankova 2014). Finally, trafficking victims particularly from Vietnam are exploited in cannabis farms. According to the National Crime Agency, in 2016 the most common type of human trafficking recorded for both adult and child (minor) victims in the UK was trafficking for the purposes of labour exploitation (NCA 2017a).[6] Some of the interviewees from law enforcement agencies and NGOs also attested to labour trafficking and exploitation commonly occurring in these sectors of work and establishments (although one needs to remember that there is often intersectionality within forms of exploitation, UK-E17; UK-E20):

---

[4]The number of sex workers in the UK is estimated to be around 72,800 with about 32,000 working in London. The EU enlargement of 2004 and 2007 had a remarkable impact on the nationalities of migrants working in prostitution in the UK (TAMPEP Network 2009). According to the Sex Work Research Hub, street-based sex workers comprise just over 25% of sex workers in the UK, with the remainder working in diverse indoor settings (cited in House of Commons—Home Affairs Committee 2016: 10).

[5]In many cases, the two forms of exploitation coincide. For example, sexual intercourse with a (trafficked) woman many times, and specifically in public and legitimate locations such as massage parlours, spas and strip clubs involves the provision of non-sexual services, e.g. a massage, a dance, serving clients, etc.

[6]At this point it should be mentioned that an individual may be recorded as a "victim of labour exploitation" although no information is provided about the sector or type of exploitation. As such, someone may be recorded as a victim of labour exploitation whether s/he is exploited in a farm, a construction site and a factory or through begging and forcing them into participating in criminal activities (e.g. cannabis farms) (see NCA 2015).

> At the age of 16, the victim, who was an orphan, was sent by his foster parents to Russia from his home in Vietnam. He stayed in Russia for 6 years, working in a restaurant. He was then told he was coming in the UK, which he was happy about. He travelled to the UK in a truck with a number of others, in a journey that lasted several days, arriving in London in August 2013. He was taken to a restaurant and worked as a waiter and pot washer, and went on to work at a clothes factory. He was given accommodation and was allowed to eat at the restaurant for free but was never paid any money. In May 2014, he was taken from London to a house in Eaglescliffe [a town in the northeast of England]. He was given some food and was told to look after some cannabis plants. He did not leave as he had been threatened and was told he still owed money to the males who took him there. (UK-E9)

Human trafficking is dispersed throughout the country and it is rather difficult to identify hotspots other than perhaps the larger cities of the UK (for sexual exploitation): London, Birmingham, Manchester, Glasgow, Newcastle, etc. However, there seems to be a significant number of (known) labour trafficking cases in the south and east of the country and a significant number of (known) sex trafficking cases in the west, the north, Wales, Scotland, and Northern Ireland (NCA 2016). It is also interesting to note that the exploitation of (the same) migrants may involve more than just the UK. Intelligence reports reveal that Albanian men and women with forged Italian passports travel to the Republic of Ireland, where they are exploited in the construction industry and in agriculture, and then move up to Northern Ireland for the same activities. In fact, they move from one country to the other on the basis of available work and for short time projects. These workers live in rented caravans or even in sheds.

Exploited individuals are controlled in a variety of ways. Workers are sometimes sold from one employer to another. Often violence and mostly threat of violence is employed. However, it is worth noting that when it comes to the sex industry in particular, competition compels entrepreneurs/traffickers to not be indiscriminately violent towards women and girls. This is not to suggest that violence is not present. The more clandestine the market, the more likely it is that there is abuse and violence (UK-E1; UK-E3; UK-4). It is also important to note that violence in the human trafficking business is often associated with specific cultural characteristics of some traffickers. For example, according to police intelligence reports, the willingness of some Chinese traffickers to use violence is seen as a method of ‘saving face’ and earning status within the trafficking collectivity rather than a rational need to control victims. In the human trafficking business there is less need for violence than in other illegal markets (e.g. drugs market, extortion/protection), and the reason, according to Kopp (2012), is the absence of a need to control a territory in the exploitation phase. This is reflected—among other—in the relatively harmonic coexistence among various small trafficking schemes in various small localities in the UK.

As regards labour trafficking—and apart from the very often clandestine nature of the phenomenon and the desperate need to earn money—there are conditions and circumstances that lead to exploitation, such as ignorance of employment and other rights in the UK, inadequate linguistic skills, and cultural issues such “acceptance of a hierarchy of family control with a fear of wider social consequences if working arrangements are challenged” (Beels 2017: 4). Recent evidence in the UK suggests that in some instances exploited individuals (especially uneducated Romanian Roma with no adequate knowledge in English) are forced into specific conditions by being threatened that if they do not comply they will be "kicked out of the country" on the basis of Brexit (e.g. UK-E9; UK-E11). In rather exceptional cases, traffickers force exploited workers to commit offences as a way of preventing them from going to the police and asking for help.

3.3 Market Structure and Social Organisation of Trafficking Networks

Reliable information on the *structures* and *operations* of trafficking networks in the UK has been less readily available as it typically depends on specific case studies (see, for example, Spencer 2014), as well as on offender profiles drawn from prosecution and conviction data. Complaints about the quality and depth of information are common, and, while this situation is typically attributed to the clandestine nature of the activity (see Surtees 2008), the involvement of a multiplicity of actors holding diverse positions towards the issue means that the process of generating relevant knowledge is not immune from important conceptual and thus, inevitably, factual biases (see Weitzer 2015; Antonopoulos and Papanicolaou 2018). Generally, the human trafficking business in the UK is fragmented and decentralised. Different actors may play a significant role in different stages of the trafficking process. These actors may:

- operate as "lone wolves" engaging/grooming vulnerable women and girls and then forcing them into prostitution. The presence of the lone trafficker is in stark contrast to the Home Office assertion that the proportion of human trafficking that is "organised" is 100% (see Mills et al. 2013);
- belong to more robust organisational forms featuring hierarchical structures. These robust organisational forms, which are rather uncommon, can be mostly found among ethnic groups with a strong familial basis such as the Albanians and typically reflect the family hierarchy;
- operate within stronger or looser networks whether as individuals, as couples or as part of smaller groups carrying out different functional activities in one or in different phases of the process. Some of these structures may operate locally and on a very small level or operate in a much wider geographic area. For example, a Polish group dismantled by the authorities operated across the UK and in cities like Edinburgh, Belfast, Glasgow, Leeds, and Newcastle. The network employed a London-based receptionist, who was effectively the person picking up the phone when a punter called and she coordinated the girls in the aforementioned localities (UK-E16).

Many trafficking collectivities operate within discrete ethnic or immigrant communities. However, cross-ethnic arrangements do exist and casual employees and/or victims are sometimes recruited from outside the core ethnic group (Webb and Burrows 2009). Chinese human traffickers, exactly because of the saturation of the Chinese restaurant/take away business in London due to the large number of Chinese, occasionally form alliances with traffickers of other nationalities in order to provide (exploitative) work for their (trafficked) compatriots. As mentioned before, and excluding the victims, there is a number of actors in human trafficking. These actors are:

- *The organiser*. The organiser is concerned with the planning of the operation, the establishment of contacts with individuals, with the recruitment of actors into a collectivity, etc. In small schemes, an organiser deals with all aspects of the schemes from recruitment and transportation to exploitation (see also Brå 2008). Very often an organiser is identified with the owner of an establishment in which the exploitation takes place. This can be, for instance, the owner of a restaurant or a car wash.
- *The recruiters*, who are concerned with the recruitment of people for sex and labour exploitation. The recruiter is someone, who lives permanently in the country of origin of the exploited individuals, and has a very good knowledge of the language, the peculiarities of each country and/or specific locale, or even knows the victims personally (UK-V1). In some instances, and in the case of sexual exploitation, ex-sex workers are used to persuade women and girls to come and work to the UK. In the case of labour exploitation, groups of workers are recruited and managed by someone of the same ethnic background. This individual acts as an intermediary between the workers and the employer and is often himself a former employee of the same employer.
- *The transporters/escorts*, who are concerned with transporting or at least assisting women in coming into the UK. There may be more than one transporter/escort throughout the whole journey, although in many cases victims (particularly from eastern Europe) for both sexual and labour exploitation travel to the UK on their own.
- *The enforcers*. In a trafficking scheme, these are individuals with the duty of supervising victims in the venues of exploitation. Many times they have the duty of collecting debts.
- *The corrupt public officials*. The corrupt public officials are those who either provide assistance during the trafficking process (e.g. employees in embassies and consulates and/or employees in local authorities) or other, who are being bribed to turn a blind eye to the exploitation (e.g. corrupt police officers).
- *The legal business owners*. These are individuals, who own the places in which the exploitation phase of the trafficking process takes place.
- *Enablers*. These can be lawyers assisting in stages of the trafficking process as well as advising and defending traffickers in a regular or ad hoc basis or professionals who are integral in the financial management of the business such as accountants (see UK-E16),
- *Freelancers*. These are facilitators that are peripherally linked to a trafficking scheme and in fact may be unaware of the scheme or the level of exploitation. These freelancers may vary from a legal business receptionist, to teenagers delivering cards for escort services to venue such as pubs, to taxi drivers and general "helpers."

The presentation of these actors within the trafficking business does not necessarily mean that these exist in every collectivity and/or scheme. It would be extremely difficult to provide an accurate profile of the trafficking group member as there seems to be a diversity of profiles rather than a profile. The individuals who participate in this business are not necessarily experienced criminals. Some have the relevant infrastructure to get involved (e.g. a legal company, a farm, a bar, a massage parlour, an apartment in which the exploitation phase takes place); some enter the business with absolutely no resources. The vast majority are men however, in some schemes the participation of women is functional (e.g. in the recruitment phase). As mentioned earlier, traffickers are not always unknown to the victims. Many times the trafficker is a friend, a neighbour, or even a member of her (nuclear or extended) family (e.g. UK-V1). The age of onset of offending is usually later than conventional criminals (late twenties/early thirties) (see also Broad 2013).

Although the belief among most of the interviewees in this study was that traffickers enter the business because it is a lucrative business ("... it's entirely motivated by significant amounts of money...", UK-E5), the reality is that there are a range of rationales for entering the market; a range of rationales that, as we will see in the next section, has financial implications:

- *Making money*: Here, there is a wide range of traffickers. Some (mostly migrant traffickers) exploit others for "survival" (see also Broad 2013), some exploit an opportunity to make money and often within the context of a legal business. In a very small number of cases minority ethnic traffickers (of British nationality) initiated small and ephemeral prostitution schemes involving underage girls in order to amass capital to start their own legitimate business (UK-E2);
- *Making money and becoming "brokers of sexual pleasure" to friends*: this is exclusively in the case of sex trafficking—"...to look like 'the man' to their friends" (UK-E2);
- *Avoiding expenses, remaining competitive, and saving their business*: this is especially the case with labour exploitation. According to the GLAA, this type of exploiters is defined as "chancer": "an individual who... knowingly or unknowingly fails to pay workers properly or give them their basic employment rights. They may start out with good intentions. They may come under pressure to reduce their margins or lose a vital contract. The chancer protects the margin of their own business by passing on an unfair share of the commercial pressure to their workers. The chancer also needs to believe that by doing the right thing by his or her employees the business is not going to be at a competitive disadvantage" (Beels 2017: 4).

Similarly to other illicit trades and activities, individuals may become involved in human trafficking via trust, familial and kinship, and neighbourhood contacts. In the case of Chinese human traffickers operating in London, associations of people with same birthplace (*tongxianghui*) are important. Finally, an environment of great importance for the formation and consolidation of relationships for human trafficking is legal businesses. Legal businesses also operate as the context in which relationships (employer–employee and between/among partners) are forged and transformed into criminal business relationships, and dependability of individuals is manifested (see also Antonopoulos and Hall 2016 for a similar trend in the illegal tobacco trade; CSD 2015).

There is discussion as to whether human traffickers are involved in other illicit trades and criminal activities. Generally, this appears to be dictated by the scale of the trafficking scheme. Small schemes tend to be specialised in sex or labour exploitation specifically, whereas large schemes or schemes associated with robust organisational forms often featuring hierarchical structures are more diversified (see NCA 2017c). These organisational forms are found to be involved in other criminal activities often violent ones (e.g. extortion and debt collection) as well as drug trafficking and counterfeiting. Intelligence reports suggest that Chinese organised crime groups operating in Strathclyde (Scotland) with links in London and Northern Ireland are involved in human trafficking for both sexual and labour exploitation as well as money lending and extortion.

3.4 Financing and Financial Management

3.4.1 Sources of Capital for Initiating/Sustaining Criminal Operations

Although, as mentioned earlier, some have the relevant infrastructure to get involved in the exploitation phase of human trafficking, generally, there are either no or very low market entry costs to the trafficking business (UK-E14; UK-E16). In the case of internal trafficking, underage victims are relatively easily recruited among groups of vulnerable people with absolutely no financial requirement being in place. In some other instances, underage vulnerable victims may be lured into sexual exploitation by small gestures like being offered a jewel, a meal, a used mobile phone, or simply being given attention and an initial nice treatment, which are unusual occurrences in their life. As one of the interviewees, who works in the field of residential child care—and among other—with vulnerable girls who have been victims of internal trafficking, mentioned:

> You don't need any money to persuade these vulnerable girls to have sex and do anything with anyone, really. Usually, we are talking about those girls who have been severely abused even by family members at a very young age, may have learning difficulties, who see the world through their 'pink glasses' and, if asked at a bus stop, a take-away, at a park, they will say 'yes, why not?'. Or girls who have been through such hardship in their life that, if you show them even the slightest interest, they are yours. Money is not essential… (UK-E13)

In the case of cross-border mobility, frequently, the "victims" have savings to migrate abroad, or have been given money by their families for trips. Naturally, in this case, no amount of money is required from traffickers. In other cases, perpetrators fund the travel of victims abroad and arrange all transportation logistics, and then use this as a form of debt-bondage when the victim has arrived to the UK. In cases in which there is a convergence between human smuggling and human trafficking, it is irregular migrants that provide the start-up capital for the business. For instance, Chinese "snakeheads" charge up to US$30,000 per head for long overland journey from east China to the UK via Russia, and eastern European countries (UK-E1; UK-E2; UK-E3; etc.). Once in the UK, many who have not paid the smuggling fees or their families are not in the position to cover the trip expenses are found work with gangmasters in order to pay for the outstanding fee. The victims themselves are sometimes manipulated into providing the capital that is needed for a trafficking scheme. One of the interviewees mentioned an interesting case in which Chinese migrants, who were to be exploited in various labour sectors in the UK, were following English language classes for which they paid their traffickers (UK-E2). Within the enlarged European Union after 2004, people come into the UK from all over Eastern Europe and in the process some may be forced to labour or sex, others may be coerced, and others are willingly "exploited" because this is the best option they have (see also Leman and Janssens 2008). Other cases involve the traffickers confiscating the identity documents from their (Eastern European) victims upon their arrival in the country, and opening bank accounts to have access to credit via overdrafts, bank loans, and credit and debit cards (see FATF/OECD 2011).

In those cases in which there is an actual investment of money in the trafficking business, the start-up capital derives from *funds from legal businesses*, and smaller or bigger savings. These legal businesses are often functional to the exploitation of trafficking victims (e.g. massage parlours, clubs, etc.) or irrelevant to the exploitation phase but useful for the trafficking process as a whole. For instance, we have come across a case in which a Lithuanian labour trafficker owned a minibus company in Lithuania. He used vehicles for the trip to the UK for £150 per person. The passengers were then introduced in labour exploitation schemes that the Lithuanian minibus company owner was a "stakeholder" (see GLA 2016b).

Sometimes money invested into human trafficking derives from *funds from other criminal activities* especially by those traffickers, who have a diversified criminal portfolio. In a rather unusual case that was described by an investigative officer working for the HMRC (Her Majesty's Revenue and Customs), the money from counterfeiting activities committed in the UK was invested in the construction of a hotel in Pakistan. The hotel was essentially an investment from proceeds of counterfeiting and facilitated a human trafficking scheme, which provided cheap labour to various businesses in the UK:

> We had information about a British Pakistani couple in Bradford. They were owners of a relatively big clothes company in Bradford and our intelligence suggested they were involved in counterfeiting. Clothes, bags, belts, you name it. We raided the premises in this area full of warehouses, and we started searching for money, products, documents. People were also working illegally in the business. One of my colleagues noticed a poster of a big building on the wall. Looked like a big house abroad but the thing is that this house was in bigger and smaller frames in their house too… In the living room, in the office, in the kitchen. Our investigation revealed that this building was in fact a hotel that was built with money from the counterfeiting business, and it was used as a recruiting and harbouring venue for trafficked persons from Asia, mostly Pakistan. After they came to the UK, they would work in the clothes company, in restaurants… (UK-E12)

3.4.1.1 Access to Capital at Critical Moments

There are a number of critical moments in the human trafficking business. These critical moments are, firstly, *business-related.* Many times, especially in relatively small localities and venues, and in relation to small schemes in the sex industry, there is a saturation point manifested in a reduced number of encounters with clients, after which the entrepreneurs must "renew" the sex workers under their control. This set of critical moments is dealt with by the creation of new cycles of sex workers in which women in a locality (or a venue) are renewed to attract clients. This system is elsewhere (Monzini 2005) referred to as a 'carousel system'. It is not unusual for women to be transported to other cities or even regions (e.g. from London to Belfast in Northern Ireland) or be exchanged (UK-E2; UK-E16; restricted intelligence reports). The system is based on pre-existing personal relationships between traffickers in the various locations and previous collaboration, not necessarily in human trafficking. Thus, the importance of social capital (i.e. connections and relationships) and symbolic capital (i.e. trust and reputation) are often more important than financial capital in sustaining a human trafficking scheme in the UK.

Secondly, critical moments in the human trafficking business are *law enforcement-related* such as, for instance, people being arrested by the authorities at UK ports and airports and/or deported or the traffickers being arrested by the authorities. These critical moments are financially covered by amounts of money that have been obtained from the business, or by the traffickers' legal business portfolios (UK-E1).

Finally, there are *miscellaneous* critical moments which may vary from the women and girls escaping, being rescued by family, friends and NGOs, being "stolen" and/or taken away by lovers; or the women/girls in the sex industry or men in labour sectors not being able to provide their sexual and/or employment "capital" (e.g. due to pregnancy, injuries, illnesses, operations, deaths). These cases, although they may cause an inconvenience, present no significant financial implication for the criminal entrepreneurs because, as mentioned earlier, there are no or very low market entry costs to the human trafficking business, and because of the large supply of (potential) victims (UK-E1; UK-E9).

3.4.2 Settlement of Payments

Payments in cash are *almost* exclusively the case in the human trafficking business for both sexual and labour exploitation. As one of the experts interviewed emphatically noted, "*the trafficking business is a cash economy... cash is king*" (UK-E9). This is also exemplified by convicted traffickers' views on asset recovery in a Home Office study (Webb and Burrows 2009). Although a number of these convicted traffickers had been aware that there might be an attempt to recover some of the money from their trafficking business, and a number of the respondents *were* (at the time of the research) subject to asset recovery processes, they did not perceive this as deterrent as most businesses were cash-based. We have not come across any cases in the UK in which credit was present in any level of the business for both sexual and labour exploitation.

Basically, there are six types of relationships between and among actors in the human trafficking business, which requires settlement of payments. These include:

1. *Trafficker to trafficker.* When there is an exchange between traffickers, e.g. selling or re-selling of women, the payment is mostly made in cash. In the case of the 'carousel system' mentioned earlier, there is no payment as such but women who are perceived as having the same "sexual capital" (UK-E1) are simply exchanged between traffickers.
2. *Trafficker to employees* in a trafficking scheme. In these cases payments are made almost exclusively in cash unless the business relationship takes place within the confines of a legal business or service. In the latter case, payments are also made electronically.
3. *Trafficker to corrupt officials.* Irrespective of the service offered to the trafficker or simply turning a blind eye to the trafficking-related activities cash is the type of payment although, occasionally, sex is provided as payment.
4. *Clients to sex workers/victims/traffickers.* In these cases payments are made predominantly in cash. Occasionally, jewels, handbags, and clothes, are gifted along with the regular payment, and this is especially the case if there is more personal relationship between the victim and a (returning) client, and in those schemes that allow some professional freedom to the sex worker (UK-E4). In extremely rare cases, especially in labour exploitation schemes, some payments are made by card directly to the owners of the legal businesses in which exploitation takes place. These are covered behind payments to legal businesses for (actual or supposed) services provided. An example that was put forward in one of the interviews involves the card payment for a package of "deluxe" cleaning services for a transportation company fleet by a cash wash (UK-E2).
5. *Traffickers/exploiters to victims.* In cases of labour exploitation, the victim's wages may be withheld entirely, thus ensuring money stays with their exploiters, or the victim receives a very meagre amount of earnings for their work. In cases of extreme exploitation (in the sex or labour markets), which constitute the ideal cases of "human trafficking," payments are made in the form of accommodation, basic amenities, clothes, and/or food (see GLA 2016b).
6. *Victims to traffickers/exploiters.* The traffickers employ various methods of ensuring payment from victims; methods which can be defined as negative, positive and administrative. The *negative* approaches, which are mostly adopted with victims who come from contexts outside the EU, include:

   - *Blackmail, violence and threat of violence* directed not only at the victim but also at family members who may be outside the UK;
   - *Juju.* This is a form of witchcraft that exists alongside Christian and Islamic beliefs predominantly in Nigeria and applies to Nigerian victims of trafficking. Within the context of juju, rituals include the taking of blood, pubic hair, etc., and swearing oaths to gods, who supposedly have power over the victims' life and death. The victims also sign contracts, which are "blessed" by juju

"priests" in Nigeria, and once at the country of destination they are under control from a distance with victims being threatened with infertility or death if clauses of the contract—including the ones relating to payments/paying back debt—are broken;

- *Economic dependency and debt bondage.* As found in other pieces of research too (e.g. Korsell et al. 2011), sex workers are expected to repay the costs for their recruitment and transportations to the destination country often at a highly inflated interest rate. Sometimes the debt bondage spills over to the victim's children:

  > I was sentenced for falsifying documents, for smuggling people and for human trafficking. I have spent almost six years in prison. I smuggled about 1,000 people… Sometimes they didn't have the money to pay you, so they'd offer you two or three children to work for you to pay their debt. They are put to work in all kinds of jobs – prostitution, stealing and construction sites. If they don't want to work, they are forced to work. (ex-trafficker quoted in HSBC 2017)

  Moreover, the wages of trafficking victims, alongside any state benefits that have been fraudulently claimed in their names, are frequently paid into bank accounts that are controlled and managed by traffickers (see NCA 2016, see also following section):

  > There were a few of us there and the trafficker who interpreted for us, but he was really there to control what we did… I never had access to my bank account… Personally, I didn't see my own bank card. Once, I stood a few metres away from a trafficker who was shuffling bank cards as if they were playing cards. There were so many of them he could barely hold them… (labour trafficking victim quoted in HSBC 2017)

- *Emotional/psychological manipulation often linked to illegal immigrant status* (e.g. UK-E11).

The *positive* approaches, which are primarily present in the sex industry, include forging business relationships based on trust. Traffickers and sex workers are seen as "partners" despite the power imbalance that exist between the two parties. Although legally this is a rather weak way of enforcing a contract in an illegal market, an agreement or a contract is signed with responsibilities for both sides, e.g. for traffickers to receive a percentage of payments earned from their victims in exchange for protection. Within this context, traffickers—as a gesture of good will, which is functional in the exploitative relationship being seen as a "partnership"—often allow sex workers to keep tips (provided by clients in addition to the normal payment for sexual services) for themselves (UK-E1; UK-E2).

Finally, the *administrative* approaches include:

- *Fines.* The fines vary significantly—they can be as little as the daily payment or as high as £2000. The latter are never paid but this process strengthens the debt bondage between a victim and the exploiter.
- *Daily quotas.* The introduction of daily quotas relieve the traffickers from the burden of having to identify ways of checking whether a sex worker, who works outdoors, steals money or does not reveal an accurate number of clients, sexual services provided and amounts of money obtained.

- "*Tie-ins*." Some employers (especially in rural areas and mostly in agriculture) keep workers' payments for 'safekeeping' supposedly in bank accounts, and deny access to these accounts (see also Skrivankova 2014). Essentially, the more an exploited individual works for such an employer, the higher the level of dependency.
- *Micro-accounting*. In many cases, especially in those in which the sex workers have some freedom (i.e. working outdoors), they are asked to report to the trafficker the number of clients they had and the amounts of money they made on a daily basis. The information in this micro-accounting process is kept in small pieces of paper. In a large sex trafficking case dealt with by the police, which involved sexual services being hidden behind (legal) massage services, transactions were recorded by the girls in diaries as "Swedish massage" (normal massage) or as "tantric massage, "which referred to sexual services offered. These diaries were used by the authorities as evidence (UK-E16).

3.4.3 Costs of Doing Business

The costs for doing business depend on a variety of factors. The scale of the trafficking scheme and its logistical complexities, the distance of the country of supply of victims, the degree of legality of the scheme, the number and types of actors involved in the business, and a number of unforeseen expenses all contribute to the costs.

Recruitment. The Internet enables traffickers to place several adverts on several sites simultaneously for free or little charge. These adverts can be posted daily and reach a very wide range of potential victims. There have been, however, cases in which victims have been bought by traffickers. Accounts that have been publicised suggest that individuals, mostly women, have been bought by traffickers for extremely small amounts of money. In a rather atypical case a vulnerable woman from a central European country was sold by her parents for £8 (UKHTC/SOCA 2013). Other amounts we came across during the research varied from £300 in some poor counties of Africa to £4000 for some women from eastern Europe. Home Office accounts also suggest that women could be purchased at UK entry points for £3000–£4000 per person, although the most quoted figure is around £700 (Webb and Burrows 2009).

Documentation expenses. Documentation is an important part of the human trafficking process especially when the victims are from non-EU member states (see Wheaton et al. 2010). According to Home Office research, passports from a variety of European countries such as the Netherlands, Norway, and Spain were bought by human traffickers for non-EU trafficked nationals for prices that ranged from £40 to £200; there was also reference to Australian passports and visas provided for £2000 (see Webb and Burrows 2009). Forged documentation costs a minimum of £850 per item in the UK. The expansion of the EU after 2004[7] cut the overheads in this type of expenses as entry could now be made on passports from the new accession states

[7] 2007 for Romania and Bulgaria.

that are generally easier to forge or acquire than those in the UK and some other popular west European destinations.[8]

Transportation/transit expenses. Expenses for travel vary on the basis of the distance involved. For those cases involving human trafficking from another geographic context into the UK, and excluding cases of legal transportation into the country, it would plausible to argue that transportation expenses are roughly similar to the (assumed) average fee for irregular migration facilitation: from Africa—£2200; from Asia—£23,800; from the Middle East—£8800; from "Other" geographic contexts—£8400 (UK Border Agency management information cited in Mills et al. 2013: 89).

Functional, exploitation-related expenses. These include expenses that are essential for the exploitation phase. When victims are based and work in one of the larger cities of the UK, such as London and Manchester, renting accommodation, such as private houses and flats can reach approximately £800–2000 per month depending on the quality and size of accommodation and area (UK-E3; UK-E4). In cases of labour exploitation, we came across cases in which small rural buildings in which as many as 10 victims were housed were rented for £300–500 per month. To these expenses victim subsistence expenses should be added. Additionally, mobile phones are often purchased as means to keep in constant contact with the victims. Pay-as-you-go sim cards, although cheap and offering a way to avoid detection, can be costly when purchased in bulk for many victims (UK-E3). Finally, in a scheme that was identified by the authorities in Scotland (the so called 'Brazilian network'), the traffickers had an appointment booking facility outsourced in London. This was basically a system which constituted a customer channel based on an online platform for which a fee was paid. The forensic accountants' investigation showed that this fee was in fact the biggest cost of the scheme (see UK-E16).

Corruption costs. It should be mentioned that corruption costs are not an integral and standard set of costs for all trafficking schemes for both sexual and labour exploitation. Traffickers/exploiters do not actively seek officials to bribe if the officials' portfolio is not essential for the scheme (e.g. travel documents) or if/when there is no knowledge of a trafficking scheme on the part of the officials. Corruption costs in human trafficking become unavoidable when officials become aware of a trafficking scheme, and in this case corruption costs are used as a type of "business insurance" by traffickers (Kugler et al. 2005). Corruption costs are reduced when payments are made in the form of sexual services rather than money (UK-E3).

Investment in the human trafficking business. One such way to invest in the business is to hire professional photographers or photography equipment to take high-quality shots of the victims that will be placed on various sex sites, as a way of maintaining a "professional" aesthetic (UK-E3; UK-E4). Similarly, some entrepreneurs

[8]The visa waiver for the new accession states practically reduced all costs related to documents for travel to zero. These costs, however, remain relevant for traffickers from other source regions—former Soviet countries, Western Balkans, Africa, Asia, etc. According to the European Border and Coast Guard Agency (FRONTEX), in 2016 the most frequently identified forged travel documents at external borders are those of Poland, Italy, Spain, and France (FRONTEX 2017).

invest in high quality escort services luxury business cards to display a sense of quality of services provided and professionalism. In a rather atypical case we came across, a Romanian trafficker invested in the physical improvement of one of his female former classmates he exploited by providing the necessary funds towards the woman having a rhinoplasty (nose plastic surgery) and a breast surgery as a way of enhancing her "marketability" (UK-E11).[9]

Payments to the victims. There is a wide range of payments on the basis of how clandestine the market is, the relationship between the trafficker and the sex worker/labourer, as well as the assumed worthiness or unworthiness of the sex worker/labourer. In those cases in which "victims" are voluntarily and knowingly recruited in a sex scheme, the sex workers receive or (to be more precise) keep 50% of their earnings. In cases in which there are significant exploitative conditions, and excluding those cases in which victims receive no payment at all, trafficking victims receive around 20% of the total turnover and sometimes as little as 2% of the revenues. For instance, some southeast European sex workers were made to earn £1000 (daily quota) but were given only £20 (UKHTC/SOCA 2013). In a case of labour exploitation in the tarmacking and block paving industry that was identified by the then Serious and Organised Crime Agency (SOCA, currently NCA), those who were considered skilled workers were paid £60–80 per day, and others who were considered workers of lower status were paid £20–30 per day (UKHTC/SOCA 2013). In cases of exploitation of vulnerable individuals, these individuals most often receive no payment at all.

Payments to other actors. As mentioned earlier, these actors are "freelancers," who are peripherally linked to a trafficking scheme and, in fact, may even be unaware of the scheme or the level of exploitation:

- managers of brothels and other (legal) venues of exploitation are paid £50–100 per shift;
- receptionists are paid £50 per shift;
- security guards working at legal businesses in which exploitation of victims takes place are paid £50 per shift;
- card boys, who deliver sex workers/escort business cards, are paid £10–20 per round;
- general helpers collecting girls and transferring them are paid £200 for each job (Webb and Burrows 2009).

Legal expenses. In the course of our research we did not come across continuous legal consultancies to human traffickers. However, when legal assistance was required, lawyers were available and their fee varied considerably depending on: the location (with London law firms charging at least three times the hourly fee as a law firm in the north of the country); how successful and able a lawyer/law firm working in criminal cases was considered; whether the services required were for contentious

---

[9]The interviewee did not provide amounts that had been invested in the surgeries. However, a rudimentary examination of prices in UK private surgeries price lists revealed that the average rhinoplasty costs approximately £3000 and a breast surgery approximately £2500.

or non-contentious work; and whether the relationship between the lawyer and the client was a long one and based on legal advice in the context of the legal business owned by the trafficker (UK-E1; UK-16).

3.4.4 *Profits and Profit Sharing*

It is often argued that the financial scale of trafficking in human beings for sexual and labour exploitation is significant with big profits for those involved (see, for example, Belser 2005). A Home Office study from the early 2000s estimated sexual exploitation at approximately £275 million in 2003 (Dubourg and Prichard 2008). Similarly, a relatively more recent study (also by the Home Office) estimated sexual exploitation of adult foreign women in the UK at around £130 million (Mills et al. 2013) on the basis of an estimated annual revenue of £48,000 per *foreign* sex worker, as put forward by Scottish Crime and Drug Enforcement Agency (SCDEA 2011) (Table 3.3).

Some indications about the financial scale of *labour* trafficking in the UK can be found in GLAA annual reports of 2013/2014, 2014/2015 and 2015/2016. From 2013 to 2016, 78 OCGs were identified or disrupted by the GLAA (and partner agencies), the worth of criminal assets identified was £18,400,000, and the amounts identified as unpaid wages, holiday pay or excessive transport charges reached £6600,000 (Table 3.4). Obviously, these figures refer to the cases known to the GLAA.

The profit margin from the human trafficking business in the UK depends on a number of variables:

- The *rationale of the entrepreneur for entering the business*. In the case of sexual exploitation, those who enter the trafficking business to make "a bit of money" and become "brokers of sex" to friends and others in their social circle tend to have the smallest profits. This is not only because these are usually people who tend to exploit a very small number of victims, generally one or two, but also because very

Table 3.3 Scale of human trafficking of foreign women for the purpose of sexual exploitation, UK by country

	Number of victims	Unit Cost (£)	Total (£ million)
England and Wales	2600	48,000	£ 120,000,000
Scotland	73	48,000	£ 4,000,000
Northern Ireland	23	48,000	£1,000,000
Total	2696		Approx. £130,000,000[a]

There is no estimate for child sexual exploitation or other forms of human trafficking in the particular report

[a]Figures may not sum due to independent rounding

Source Project Acumen and Northern Ireland Organised Crime taskforce cited in Mills et al. (2013: 86), SCDEA (2011)

Table 3.4 OCGs identified/disrupted, worth of criminal assets identified and amount identified as unpaid wages holiday pay or excessive transport charges, GLAA investigations (2013–2016)

	OCGs identified/disrupted	Worth of criminal assets identified (£)	Amounts identified as unpaid wages, holiday pay or excessive transport charges
2013–2014	10	900,000	1,700,000
2014–2015	32	5,100,000	3,500,000
2015–2016	36	12,400,000[a]	1,400,000
Summary 2013–2016	78	18,400,000	6,600,000

[a]Affected by one substantial case
Sources compiled from GLA (2014, 2015, 2016a)

often they do not accept money for the sexual services which their victims provide; the position they have in their social circle as sex brokers is more important. In the case of trafficking for labour exploitation, those who enter the business in order to save expenses from the working of their legal business with the goal to save their business have no significant profits. Generally, the biggest profits come to those who are geared towards making significant profits, are diversified in their predatory activities, and are willing to exploit their victims in more than one ways. In some cases the latter type of traffickers' profits made from the sexual and/or labour exploitation of the victims are supplemented by profits from additional activities for which the victims' identities and family circumstances are essential. Firstly, these traffickers run into debt the victims' bank accounts. After their arrival in the UK, the victims are not given the promised job for weeks or even months. This makes them completely dependent on their traffickers for their living expenses, and in this way debt is built up since traffickers pay for/or provide accommodation and food. This debt is often used as leverage on victims to open bank accounts so that they can apply for jobs and once the bank debit card is sent, it is kept by the traffickers and used to withdraw relatively small amounts of cash from ATMs. Secondly, traffickers obtain loans in the victims' names. This is especially the case in labour exploitation cases. This also creates a situation in which the victims think twice about leaving the trafficker/gangmaster and starting a new life with heavy debts. Thirdly, traffickers (especially east Europeans) get child benefits for the victims' children, who live in their country of origin, as well as working tax credit for each (exploited) worker, which is approximately £2000 per worker per year (see GLA 2016b).

- The *number of victims exploited by a trafficking scheme.* According to Belser (2005), the accurate estimation of the profits from trafficking (π) results from multiplying the total number of the trafficking victims by the average turnover from each victim (the value-added, VA) minus total wage payments or other expenses (W): $\pi = VA - W$. Naturally, the bigger the number of the victims exploited by a trafficking scheme, the higher the profits (UK-E16).

- *Vulnerability* and *"quality" of the victims*. Vulnerability of trafficking victims generally means that payments to these victims are either low or non-existent resulting in a bigger profit margin for the trafficker. In fact, many of the victims are not even aware of financial transactions taking place between someone, who has sex with her and a trafficker/exploiter (UK-V1). The same applies to labour exploitation. Victims of labour exploitation with mental health problems, for instance, are either not paid at all or paid insignificant amounts of money.
- *The embeddedness of the exploitation phase of trafficking in a legal business*. Trafficking profits are related to the *modus operandi* of the traffickers, and the interaction of the victims, actors in the trafficking collectivities and, of course, the client, during the exploitation phase. Sexual intercourse with a trafficked woman many times, especially when it is embedded in a legal business (e.g. massage parlour, spa, club), is not only the result of a procedure in which the prospective client approaches the trafficker and/or the woman (or vice versa). It involves a number of steps of financial significance. It was noted earlier that trafficked women are introduced to street and brothel prostitution or prostitution that is covered behind the provision of other services in bars, clubs and massage parlors. Some of the money that traffickers get in the non-street and non-brothel prostitution is a product of the labour of women and not of the exploitation of the women's sexuality per se. For instance, many times a *massage* (the legal service in a massage parlor relating to labour) may lead to *sexual intercourse* (the illegal service relating to the exploitation of sexuality of women). In this case, sexual services are the reason why people received non-sexual services too. In many cases, clients are obliged to consume a certain amount of drinks or certain types of drinks (e.g. champagne) before the provision of the sexual services. Profits from trafficking of women for commercial sex that take place in legal business settings include profits from the *labour* exploitation of the women too (ℓ): to slightly enhance Belser's (2005) formula, $\pi = (VA - W) + \ell$. Importantly, the embeddedness of a human trafficking scheme in a legal business allows for the reduction of costs for the trafficking scheme.
- Whether *loans* are lent with sometimes logical, sometimes irrational interest rates in the process of migrating in the UK. According to some traffickers, in many cases in which women knew which labour sector they were going to be involved and, in fact, actively sought entry to the UK sex market, the women had accepted the facilitation fee as their own debt. Traffickers would lend £1000 to the women to travel to the UK and the women would then be expected to pay £1500 from their work in the sex industry (Webb and Burrows 2009).

Spending and investing human trafficking profits. In most cases of trafficking in the UK, profits are simply spent on lifestyle expenses, jewels, holidays, gifts for girlfriends, and cars. According to GLA (2016b), traffickers may use the victims' names for car tax and insurance so that the cars are not tracked to the traffickers. Significant parts of the profits are used to paying off debts incurred by the traffickers and their families and friends. Profits are also invested in the legal economy and specifically in cash intensive businesses (that are often identified as venues of exploitation) such as fast food restaurants, car washes, nail bars, and beauty salons. Sums of money are used for property purchases in the UK and in the country of origin of non-British traffickers (UK-E9; UK-E14; UK-E16; UK-E20; Box 3.1). Rarely, trafficking profits are used towards the expansion of the business. The more clandestine the scheme, the more difficult it is for this scheme to be expanded; schemes that are embedded in legal business are more likely to be invested upon.

Box 3.1. Proceeds of labour trafficking: The case of Stasys Skarbalius and Virginija Skarbaliene

Stasys Skarbalius and Virginija Skarbaliene operated as gangmasters illegally between 2006 and 2010 after fraudulently setting up Scunthorpe-based business CV Staff Services. They did it under a fake identity and in turn applied for licences from the Gangmasters Licensing Authority (GLA) and mortgages to build a property portfolio. During this time, they facilitated hundreds of people into work in the agricultural and horticultural industries in Lincolnshire and Humberside, across Yorkshire, Suffolk, Norfolk and Cambridge. Off the profits of the business, which had an estimated turnover of £12 million, they lived lavish lifestyles. The sham was exposed in 2011 when Skarbalius' bogus Dutch passport, which he held under the name of Charles Rene Luske, expired and he was unable to renew it for the purposes of the annual licence.

Both of no fixed address, Skarbalius, aged 62, was jailed for two-and-a-half years and Skarbaliene, aged 58, received three years. They were also disqualified as company directors for seven years. Sheffield Crown Court heard how they had each received total benefits of £1 million from their criminal exploits. They were served with Confiscation Orders under the Proceeds of Crime Act on their available assets—£187,219.85 for Skarbalius and £231,687.68 for Skarbaliene. Included in their assets are substantial bank account balances, recovered cash, a Mercedes Sprinter van, a Lexus Sport, a Volkswagen Transporter van, their four-bedroom detached home in Scotter, Lincolnshire, two three-bedroom houses occupied by tenants in Scunthorpe, and their Scunthorpe business premises.

Source: GLAA website

Money laundering and movement of trafficking proceeds. Money laundering on a sophisticated, complex and systematic scale was not a common practice identified in our research. Illicit profits were used to establish licit business interests insofar as this may be regarded as money laundering. However, illicit proceeds were not subsequently laundered through these legal businesses once they had been established. There have been, however, cases reported in which traffickers involved in small trafficking schemes laundered their money via simple fraudulent child welfare benefits schemes (see also Sect. 3.5 in this chapter). In a rather exceptional case, MX, a Chinese "madam" who ran a series of brothels across north London, purportedly had had strong links to the Triads, and was involved in sex trafficking and drug trafficking, was convicted for money laundering (intelligence case provided in Hutton 2017).

With regard to the movement of trafficking money out of the UK, the general perception during the course of the research was that because of the fragmentation of the business, there is not much need to move money internationally. When there is movement of trafficking money, legal financial institutions are used. In cases of east European traffickers, there has been some repatriation of funds through bank transfer of small amounts that do not alert the authorities and which have "…nothing extravagantly sophisticated about it" (UK-E16). One of the interviewees referred to a ROCU (Regional Organised Crime Unit) investigation into a Chinese criminal organisation which transferred millions of pounds by a number of banks in the UK to Hong Kong. The bank accounts, which were in different locations in the country, were linked to brothels. It was estimated that between £5–15 million were transferred to Hong Kong (UK-E14). However, usually instant money transfer services such as MoneyGram or Western Union, in which small deposits are made at a time, are used by traffickers. In this case, money from the trafficking business is transferred to the country of origin of the traffickers and sent to extended family members and friends (large number of recipients) (see also Broad 2013). The Brazilian network mentioned earlier, used the Telecom 2 Surf and Pay facility, a secure web-based credit card payment gateway solution, to process their online spending; a significant portion of the expenditure was in Brazil. They also used the NatWest (National Westminster Bank) remittance service to repatriate cash sums back to Brazil (UK-E16). Finally, in those cases in which women are collected at UK entry points and purchased on the spot, transporters/escorts are paid in cash, and money is immediately *physically* transported back into the originating country (see Webb and Burrows 2009).

3.5 The Role and Impact of the Internet on Human Trafficking Activities and Finances

The internet (and ICT in general) has affected the business models of traffickers in all phases of the trafficking process as well as the financial aspects of their activities. With regard to *recruitment*, a plethora of websites, including social networking and microblogging services such as Facebook and Twitter, as well as online classifieds, dating and international marriage agency sites, have been documented as recruiting people into trafficking, for the purposes of sexual or labour exploitation, along with offline forms of recruitment, such as word-of-mouth, or through friends and relatives. To lure and recruit victims online, traffickers frequently place spurious, promising advertisements on employment, dating and marriage websites for jobs including administration, cleaning, home help, child and older people care, waitressing, hostessing, pole dancing, the collection and delivery of charity bags, agricultural farming and construction roles, educational courses or work in the tourism sector (UK-E1; UK-E2; UK-E3; UK-E4; UK-E5; UK-E18, etc. see also Europol 2014).

Direct contact is also initiated with victims in chat rooms or via social networking sites, where traffickers pose as friends or lovers to recruit victims, often exchanging e-mails, messages, photographs and videos with their victims to build a relationship and gain their trust and confidence (see also Diba et al. 2017).

Another interesting point raised in the interviews concerns the usage of social media applications by sex traffickers to determine the proximity of a potential victim to them, in terms of a nearby town or city, or even within the same locality, thus enabling them to easily track, meet and build up a relationship to gain the targeted victim's trust. Many electronic devices such as mobile phones and tablets have, within their settings, built-in location services functions that enable any third-party applications and websites to use information based on the user's current location, and to provide numerous location-based services, such as finding nearby amenities that include parks and restaurants. On this point, if a user has enabled location services, knowingly or unknowingly, on their device, then such action would allow social media applications, such as Facebook and/or Twitter to gain access to and publicly display the user's location to their "friends," through the user's status updates, uploading of photographs and messages sent via Facebook's Messenger feature or, depending on the user's privacy settings, whoever is able to view their profile. Consequently, the visibility of one's location to others can have negative implications for the user, and possess much benefit for a trafficker searching for women to recruit. NGO representatives interviewed by Diba et al. (2017) mentioned that many of the victims they had worked with were not shrewd in their use of the internet and were neglectful in checking their location services settings on their mobile phones. Finally, with regard to the recruitment phase, the Internet has allowed not only the easier identification of potential victims but also additional opportunities for profits at this phase. In one case of labour exploitation, for instance, potential victims from Lithuania were recruited via a Lithuanian website and paid £350 each to the trafficker, who managed the particular website to secure a job in the UK (UKHTC/SOCA 2013).

The internet has also facilitated *the transportation* of trafficking victims. Social media sites have been used to aid the transportation process by, among other, facilitating the booking of tickets and obtaining travel documentation in several types of transportation. Tickets are purchased online by traffickers often by using compromised credit card data, in order to conceal their identities and, thereby, add another layer of anonymity and distance to their criminal proceedings. Furthermore, the use of stolen credit card information beneficially ensures that neither the tickets nor the victims are able to be easily linked back to the traffickers (Diba et al. 2017). Digital technologies enable counterfeiting as better fake documents essential for the trip are developed at reduced prices (UK-E3).

With regard to *exploitation*, the ICTs has also augmented the nature of sex work from a predominantly physical environment to an increasingly virtual landscape to such an extent that most prostitution is currently advertised and solicited online, in what has been referred to in the literature as "virtual red light districts" (Cauduro et al. 2009: 59). Correspondingly, there has been a significant shift in human trafficking activity for the purposes of sexual exploitation to the virtual sphere, with both the supply and demand side having benefitted from the use of the Internet and digital technologies, with trafficked victims often being advertised online (see Diba et al. 2017). Naturally, ICTs have elevated risks of detection of trafficking schemes. Adverts can be captured via screenshots, with "digital traces" being left such as remnants of old/expired adverts. As a means to counteract residual criminal activity, one very common pattern adopted by traffickers is the repeated posting of adverts, often several times a day for a week, then all of the adverts being closed. After a few weeks, again, several adverts are then placed and repeatedly advertised with the listed women being featured under new aliases and often, different locations, which would signify repeated movement across cities in the UK (UK-E2; UK-E3; UK-E16).

The financial implication of the use of the internet and ICTs for human trafficking is that, firstly, the costs for recruitment are minimised. The research found that spurious job advertisements are placed on various employment, dating and marriage websites at the same time to lure and recruit potential victims for free. Websites are often created by traffickers in the countries of origin and in the languages of potential victims, with one site linking to another, building international recruitment networks. As such, the content on the first site can be used as a template, and the same layout can be used over and over again, and translated into the different languages of the sex markets where the traffickers desire to trade. ICTs have also reduced costs that are related to the control of victims in the exploitation phase:

> 20 years ago a trafficker would require someone to look out for the girls. This is not necessary any more, at least not to that extent… (UK-E3; UK-E1).

In addition, ICT have led to some changes in the facilitation of the business and on spending patterns by traffickers in some trafficking schemes. The 'Brazilian network' mentioned earlier, used a system based on an online platform to handle customers as well as a secure web-based credit card payment gateway to process their on online spending in Brazil (UK-E16). However, the general consensus among the participants in the current research was that when it comes to financial aspects linked to the exploitation phase "ICT… means leaving a trace, and this is against the logic of this illegal market" (UK-E8; also UK-E15; UK-16, etc.).

3.6 Conclusion

Understanding the broader range of financial aspects of human trafficking is an important component of the process of crimes for gain and can contribute to more effective investigation and prevention (see also Antonopoulos et al. 2015; Levi 2013). However, despite the fact that "proceeds of crime" and "tackling criminal finances" have been a priority for policymakers and law enforcement agencies in the UK (and internationally) (see, for example, HM Government 2015), there is "low level financial intelligence captured" (UK-E16) and relatively little is known about the financial management of human trafficking in the country.

Human trafficking data in the UK are unreliable, and apart from technical reasons (e.g. dark figure, dependency on actions by the authorities, identifying *potential* victims, etc.) this is because these data are often produced with an eye to isolating human trafficking from the illegal and legal economic activities trafficking facilitates (see Kopp 2012).

Our research has shown that the human trafficking scene in the UK is extremely fragmented and with a low entry threshold. In those cases in which there is investment in a trafficking scheme, the start-up capital derives from funds from legal businesses and savings and/or funds from other criminal activities especially for those traffickers who have a diversified criminal portfolio. Payments in cash are almost exclusively the case in the human trafficking business; the exceptions are some transactions that take place within the confines of a legal business or payments in kind (e.g. provision of free sex to corrupt officials). The traffickers employ a variety of negative, positive and administrative methods to ensure payment from victims.

The costs for doing business depend on the scale of the trafficking scheme and its logistical complexities, the distance of the country of supply of victims, the degree of legality of the scheme and its possible embeddedness in a legal business, the number and types of actors involved, and a number of unforeseen expenses in critical moments. The profits depend on the trafficker's rationale for entering the business, the number of victims exploited, the vulnerability and (perceived) "quality"/worthiness of the victims, the embeddedness of the exploitation phase in a legal business, and the presence of loans to victims.

Although some significant amounts have been laundered in *specific* cases, generally, sophisticated laundering schemes are the exception rather than the rule in the UK. The management of profits from human trafficking reflects primarily the fragmented nature of the phenomenon, the relatively small size of most schemes, the financial abilities of the criminal entrepreneurs and possible embeddedness of a trafficking scheme in a legal business, as well as the traffickers' personal circumstances. Investments are modest (reflecting in most cases the modest profits made in a rather open and highly competitive business), and apart from property, traffickers invest in cash-intensive businesses.

Continuous development of the knowledge base on the social organisation of human trafficking and its financial aspects is necessary. Finances are not just another element of the human trafficking process but are integrally linked to the social organisation of the phenomenon from recruitment to exploitation. In addition, there is a need for research to be done on the rationale of human traffickers for entering the business. Considering "getting money" as simply the rationale for entering (and staying) in the business offers a partial and incomplete view. Moreover, there is a need for continuous development of the knowledge base on the ways ICTs have been impacting on the social organisation and finances of the particular business. In the online sphere, a few years can be an era in terms of developments.

References

Antonopoulos, G. A., & Hall, A. (2016). The financial management of the illicit tobacco trade in the United Kingdom. *British Journal of Criminology, 56*(4), 709–728.

Antonopoulos, G. A., Hall, A., Levi, M., & Rusev, A. (2015). Understanding Criminal Finances: Policy and Methodological Framework. In CSD (Ed.), *Financing of organised crime* (pp. 11–28). Sofia: CSD.

Antonopoulos, G. A., & Papanicolaou, G. (2018). *Organised crime: A very short introduction*. Oxford: Oxford University Press.

Beels, M. (2017). *Preventing labour exploitation*. Warwick Papers in Industrial Relations n. 107. Coventry: University of Warwick.

Belser, P. (2005). *Forced labor and human trafficking: Estimating the profits*. Working Paper 42. Geneva: International Labor Office.

Brå. (2008). *The organisation of human trafficking*. Stockholm: Brå.

Brayley, H., & Cockbain, E. (2014). British children can be trafficked too: Towards an inclusive definition of internal child sex trafficking. *Child Abuse Review, 23*(3), 171–184.

Broad, R. (2013). *Stuck in traffic: A study of individuals convicted for human trafficking offences through the UK Criminal Justice System*. Doctoral thesis, School of Law, University of Manchester.

Cauduro, A., Di Nicola, A., Fonio, C., Nuvoloni, A., & Ruspini, P. (2009). Innocent when you dream: Clients and trafficked women in Italy. In A. Di Nicola, A. Cauduro, M. Lombardi, & P. Ruspini (Eds.), *Prostitution and human trafficking. Focus on clients* (pp. 31–66). New York: Springer.

CSD. (2015). *Financing of organised crime*. Sofia: Centre for the Study of Democracy.

Cockbain, E. (2018). *Offender and victim networks in human trafficking*. London: Routledge.

Diba, P., Antonopoulos, G. A., & Papanicolaou, G. (2017). *Surf and sound—The role of the internet in the human smuggling and trafficking process: UK report*. Middlesbrough: Teesside University & European Commission.

Dubourg, R., & Prichard, S. (2008). *Organised crime: revenues, economic and social costs, and criminal assets available for seizure*. London: Home Office.

Europol. (2014). *Trafficking in human beings and the internet*. The Hague: Europol.

FATF/OECD. (2011). *Money laundering risks arising from trafficking in human and smuggling of migrants*. Paris: FATF.

FRONTEX. (2017). *Risk analysis for 2017*. Warsaw: FRONTEX.

Gadd, D., Broad, R., Craven, J., Lightowlers, C., & Bellotti, E. (2017). *Mapping the contours of modern slavery in Greater Manchester*. Manchester: Centre for Criminology and Criminal Justice.

GLA. (2014). *GLA annual report and accounts, 1 April 2013 to 31 March 2014*. Nottingham: GLA.

GLA. (2015). *GLA Annual report and accounts, 1 April 2014 to 31 March 2015*. Nottingham: GLA.

GLA. (2016a). *GLA annual report and accounts, 1 April 2015 to 31 March 2016*. Nottingham: GLA.

GLA. (2016b). *Horse trading*. Available online at: https://www.youtube.com/watch?v=k-I5EtcewdM.

Goodey, J. (2008). Human trafficking: Sketchy data and policy responses. *Criminology and Criminal Justice, 8*, 421–442.

Harris, D., Sheehan, J., Toft, A., & Weatherburn, A. (2014). *Severe forms of labour exploitation, UK 2014*. Nottingham: University of Nottingham.

Haughey, C. (2016). *The modern slavery act review*. https://www.gov.uk/government/uploads/system/uploads/attachment_data/file/542047/2016_07_31_Haughey_Review_of_Modern_Slavery_Act_-_final_1.0.pdf.

HM Government. (2015). *The serious and organised crime strategy: Annual report for 2014*. London: HMSO.

Home Office. (2009). *Extending our reach: A comprehensive approach to tackling serious organised crime*. London: The Stationery Office.

Home Office. (2014). *Review of the National Referral Mechanism for victims of human trafficking*. London: Home Office.

Hornsby, R., Harvey, J., & Booth, D. (2017). Trafficked, smuggled or exploited: Ignore the labels, they all involve abuse. In P. C. van Duyne, J. Harvey, G. A. Antonopoulos, & K. von Lampe (Eds.), *The many faces of crime for profit and ways of tackling it* (pp. 325–348). Nijmegen: Wolf Legal Publishers.

House of Commons—Home Affairs Committee. (2016). *Prostitution: Third report of session 2016–2017*. London: House of Commons.

HSBC. (2017). *Challenging the human traffickers*. Available online at: http://www.hsbc.com/news-and-insight/insight-archive/2017/challenging-the-human-traffickers.

Hutton, S. (2017). *Organised crime: An ethnographic study of the monitoring and disrupting of those designated as high-level 'organised criminals' within the metropolitan police*. Unpublished Ph.D. thesis, Open University.

Kelly, L., & Regan, L. (2000). *Stopping traffic: Exploring the extent of, and responses to, trafficking in women for sexual exploitation in the UK*. Police Research Series Paper 125. London: Home Office.

Kopp, P. (2012). Human trafficking and international financial flows. In P. Reuter (Ed.), *Draining development: Controlling flow of illicit funds from developing countries* (pp. 171–202). Washington, DC: World Bank Press.

Korsell, L., Vesterhav, D., & Skinnari, J. (2011). Human trafficking and drug distribution in Sweden from a market perspective—Similarities and differences. *Trends in Organised Crime, 14*(2–3), 100–124.

Kugler, M., Verdier, T., & Zenou, Y. (2005). Organised Crime, Corruption and Punishment. *Journal of Public Economics, 89*(9–10), 1639–1663.

Leman, J., & Janssens, S. (2008). The Albanian and post-Soviet business of trafficking women for prostitution: Structural developments and financial modus operandi. *European Journal of Criminology, 5*(4), 433–451.

Levi, M. (2013). *Drug law enforcement and financial investigation practices* (Report n. 5). London: International Drug Policy Consortium.

Mills, H., Skodbo, S., & Blyth, P. (2013). *Understanding organised crime: Estimating the scale and the social and economic costs*. London: Home Office.

Monzini, P. (2005). *Sex traffic*. London: Zed.

National Audit Office. (2017). *Reducing modern slavery*. London: National Audit Office.

NCA. (2015). *NCA strategic assessment: The nature and scale of human trafficking in 2014*. London: NCA.

NCA. (2016). *National strategic assessment of serious and organised crime 2016*. Available online at: http://www.nationalcrimeagency.gov.uk/publications/731-national-strategic-assessment-of-serious-and-organised-crime-2016/file.

NCA. (2017a). *Human trafficking: National Referral Mechanism statistics—End of year summary 2016*. Available online at: http://www.nationalcrimeagency.gov.uk/publications/national-referral-mechanism-statistics/2016-nrm-statistics/788-national-referral-mechanism-statistics-end-of-year-summary-2016/file.

NCA. (2017b). *National Referral Mechanism (NRM)*. Available online at: http://www.nationalcrimeagency.gov.uk/about-us/what-we-do/specialist-capabilities/uk-human-trafficking-centre/national-referral-mechanism.

NCA. (2017c). *National strategic assessment of serious and organised crime 2017*. Available online at: http://www.nationalcrimeagency.gov.uk/publications/807-national-strategic-assessment-of-serious-and-organised-crime-2017/file.

Oram, S., Khondoker, M., Abas, M., Broadbent, M., & Howard, L. M. (2015). Characteristics of trafficked adults and children with severe mental illness: A historical cohort study. *The Lancet Psychiatry, 2*(12), 1084–1091.

Project Acumen. (2010). *Setting the record: The trafficking of migrant women in the England and Wales off-street prostitution sector*. London: ACPO.
Salt, J., & Stein, J. (1997). Migration as a business: The case of trafficking. *International Migration, 35,* 467–493.
SCDEA. (2011). *Human trafficking intelligence assessment summary*. Paisley: SCDEA.
Silverman, B. (2014). *Modern slavery: An application of multiple systems estimation*. Available online at: https://www.gov.uk/government/uploads/system/uploads/attachment_data/file/386841/Modern_Slavery_an_application_of_MSE_revised.pdf.
Skrivankova, K. (2014). *Forced labour in the United Kingdom*. York: Joseph Rowntree Foundation.
Spencer, J. (2014). Human trafficking policy making and the politics of international criminal justice: A case study of sexual exploitation. In P. C. van Duyne, J. Harvey, G. A. Antonopoulos, K. von Lampe, A. Maljević, & A. Markovska (Eds.), *Corruption, greed and crime-money: Sleaze and shady economy in Europe and beyond* (pp. 291–312). Nijmegen: Wolf Legal Publishers.
Surtees, R. (2008). Traffickers and trafficking in Southern and Eastern Europe. Considering the other side of human trafficking. *European Journal of Criminology, 5,* 39–68.
TAMPEP Network. (2009). *Sex work in Europe: A mapping of the prostitution Scene in 25 European countries*. Amsterdam: TAMPEP.
The Guardian. (2016, October 12). Police not recording most UK slavery cases as crimes, says report. *The Guardian*.
UKHTC/SOCA. (2013). *A strategic assessment on the scale and nature of human trafficking in 2012*. Available online at: http://www.nationalcrimeagency.gov.uk/publications/15-ukhtc-strategic-assesssment-on-human-trafficking-in-2012/file.
UNODC. (2009). *Trafficking in persons: Analysis on Europe*. Vienna: UNODC.
Webb, S., & Burrows, J. (2009). *Organised immigration crime: A post-conviction study*. Research Report 15. London: Home Office.
Weitzer, R. (2012). Sex trafficking and the sex industry: The needs for evidence-based theory and legislation. *Journal of Criminal Law and Criminology, 101*(4), 1337–1370.
Weitzer, R. (2015). Human trafficking and contemporary slavery. *Annual Review of Sociology, 41,* 223–242.
Wheaton, E. M., Schauer, E. J., & Galli, T. V. (2010). Economics of human trafficking. *International Migration, 48*(4), 114–141.
Zhang, S. (2009). Beyond the Natasha story—A review and critique of current research on sex trafficking. *Global Crime, 10*(3), 178–195.

Conclusion

Keywords Human trafficking · Crime money · Financial management · Hawala · Information and communication technologies

On the basis of the available evidence from the three European contexts examined in this book, Bulgaria, Italy and the United Kingdom, a number of observations can be made. To begin with, the criminal structures involved vary substantially. Generally, the market is dominated by sole 'players', small-to-medium (often family-based) organisations and loosely structured networks, whereas highly organised, hierarchical groups are rather an exception. Human trafficking besides being a heinous crime is a criminal market, which generates substantial profits. The related costs of and profits from human trafficking vary substantially depending on the modus operandi of perpetrators, the victims' countries of origin and destination, as well as the particular market sector or segment in which the victims are exploited.

Low entry costs generally apply to domestic and intra-community trafficking in EU and in cases where perpetrators control a small number of victims. 'Lover-boys' exploiting one or two victims in prostitution are a typical example, and they work either outdoors or in the lower segments of in-door prostitution acquiring customers online. Costs might be particularly high in those cases in which victims are exploited in contexts that are geographically distant to their country of origin. In such cases, beyond paying for transportation costs, there are added expenses such as corruption payments to officials, and securing forged documentation. Despite the fact that these expenses are usually imposed as a debt onto the victim and, subsequently, are more or less quickly recovered by the traffickers, the money has to be invested by traffickers on forehand in order to ensure that victims can reach the destination. In addition, extra start-up costs can be required, especially in prostitution markets, if traffickers want to pursue more profitable locations, which guarantee steady and higher revenue.

It appears that trafficking for labour exploitation is less demanding than sexual exploitation in terms of market entry threshold and operational costs, and it also involves lower risks of detection and criminal sanctions. Traffickers operating

G. A. Antonopoulos et al., *Human Trafficking Finances*, SpringerBriefs in Criminology, https://doi.org/10.1007/978-3-030-17809-3

internationally within EU and domestic traffickers have the competitive advantage of low transportation costs and absence of visa and labour restrictions. With regard to trafficking for sexual exploitation this has obvious impact on their business models. Thus, East European traffickers more often tend to spend money for acquiring access to more lucrative locations such as red light district windows, brothels and massage parlours, and in the end harness higher profits. Conversely, for Nigerian, Latin American and Chinese networks transportation costs (including costs to obtain travel and residence documents) occur to predominate their expenses.

The observed differences in cost structure and cost-benefit ratios are part of the explanation why Bulgaria and Romania still remain among the top countries of origin of victims, despite having much smaller population than Nigeria or China. These differences also offer insights into the preferred modus operandi of traffickers in terms of exerting control. Eastern Europeans enjoy lower start-up costs and relatively higher revenue and thus more often rely on building business-like relations with exploited sex workers, wherein they would secure more profitable locations and share part of the revenue with the victims. The relative geographical proximity of Western Europe and free movement practically render controlling routes of migration obsolete, so Eastern European traffickers rather focus on controlling access to profitable locations. On the opposite, the high transportation costs, entry, labour and residence restrictions for third country nationals turn control over routes of migration into the primary 'asset' of traffickers from these regions. Arguably, this provides a possible explanation why traffickers from Africa and Asia more often rely on debt bondage and tend to withhold all or the bulk of the earnings of their victims. The above arguments are also largely applicable to cases related to both trafficking for sexual and labour exploitation.

Settlement of payments in human trafficking remains largely cash-based. This is true for practically all types of transactions in cases related to sexual exploitation—from customer to sex worker, from sex worker to trafficker, between different participants in trafficking networks and between traffickers and possible intermediaries. Less frequently, payments to intermediaries and associates might be made in kind, or customers might pay through credits cards under the pretext of paying for other services (e.g. massage). In the case of labour trafficking settlement of payments depends on the cash-intensity of the sector which the workers are exploited in. However, even in sectors in which bank transfers are the norm, usually workers' accounts are controlled by traffickers and their wages are immediately withdrawn in cash.

In terms of the money laundering techniques, the present analysis shows that these are most often rudimentary. Most traffickers use the bulk of the proceeds to sustain a lavish lifestyle and spend profits on luxury goods, partying, vacations etc. When there is a surplus, it is often invested into real estate and expensive vehicles. More sophisticated trafficking networks, which retain larger portions of the profit, also invest in different cash intensive businesses in home countries. Proceeds are also used to cover running costs of the existing trafficking operation and may sometimes be channelled to an expansion of the business. A notable recent tendency for Bulgarian traffickers are investments for acquiring or long-term renting of adult clubs and other sex venues in the destination countries. However, the data indicates that investment into other illicit enterprises is rare.

Foreign traffickers operating abroad tend to transfer all profit surpluses from the destination to their country of origin. Transportation of cash is a particularly popular method, carried out either by the traffickers themselves, victims, or associates. Money transfer companies are also employed, although the observed recent trend rather indicates that traffickers resort to such companies less often due to the easy traceability of transactions. In order to minimize risks of detection and hinder any possible investigations, the money is first broken down to smaller sums and then transferred not by traffickers but by others, i.e. victims, associates, friends, family or intermediaries. Bank transfers are generally avoided and in case they are employed, similar risk minimization techniques are used. Some traffickers also employ one or more shell companies to facilitate money laundering. Alternatively, a trade-based technique might be implied with diverse goods being purchased in the country of exploitation and subsequently be resold in the country of origin of traffickers. Trafficking networks from Asia and Africa also widely employ hawala or similar informal value transfer systems to move their proceeds from the countries where they exploit the victims to their home countries. In this case money does not cross borders physically and the transactions are based on established relations of trustworthiness of the participants in the Hawala network.

The Internet (and ICT in general) is used in numerous ways to facilitate human trafficking and its financial management. On one hand, recruitment can be carried out online or supplemented through online communication. In the case of the trafficking for sexual exploitation, the Internet also presents a useful platform for advertising the services offered by the victims and is actively used by both organised criminal groups and independent traffickers. In addition, the Internet can present an additional medium of control over victims, whose communication and agreements with clients can be monitored. On the other hand, it allows independent traffickers and sex workers to operate and acquire customers without having to pay for costly work spaces. Thus, the Internet generally represents a cost-effective way to initiate, facilitate or even sustain a trafficking operation. The downside of the new technologies is the heightened visibility, hence the higher risk of detection and apprehension by law enforcement authorities, as well as increased vulnerability to competitors. Nonetheless, the biggest change that new technologies and the Internet have brought about, especially in the case of trafficking for sexual exploitation, is that they have put sole players and more sophisticated criminal structures on equal foot.

Our research begins to draw attention to the financial management of human trafficking. The ambition is that our investigation will be used as an important building block for further research on this neglected aspect of the particular criminal business.

Index

G. A. Antonopoulos et al., *Human Trafficking Finances*, SpringerBriefs
in Criminology, https://doi.org/10.1007/978-3-030-17809-3

The manufacturer's authorised representative in the EU is Springer Nature Customer Service Centre GmbH, Europaplatz 3, 69115 Heidelberg, Germany. If you have any concerns regarding our products, please contact ProductSafety@springernature.com

Printed and bound by CPI Group (UK) Ltd, Croydon, CR0 4YY
05/10/2026
02228152-0007